Raccoon

Raccoon

Daniel Heath Justice

REAKTION BOOKS

To Rachel Poliquin and all the AnimalFest 2015 authors,
whose shared love of these beasts and these books
inspired me to write another one

Published by
REAKTION BOOKS LTD
Unit 32, Waterside
44–48 Wharf Road
London N1 7UX, UK
www.reaktionbooks.co.uk

First published 2021
Copyright © Daniel Heath Justice 2021

Printed and bound in India by Replika Press Pvt. Ltd.

A catalogue record for this book is available from the British Library

ISBN 978 1 78914 424 6

Contents

Introduction:
An Uncanny Outlaw

Both in expression and in movement, she showed that strange
mixture of gaiety, ferocity, mischievousness, and confident
sagacity, which makes the raccoon unlike in character to all
the other wild kindreds.
Charles G. D. Roberts, *The Watchers of the Trails*[1]

Black masks, striped tails, nimble fingers and quick minds: raccoons are instantly recognizable even in locales where they are
known only in captivity or popular culture. For centuries they have
been native icons of wild America, although today they are increasingly associated with human-dominated cityscapes. Long before
the spacefaring bandit Rocket Raccoon found global popularity
in the Marvel Cinematic Universe, his four-legged counterparts
were making regular if largely stereotyped appearances in
Hollywood films and cartoons, alongside those in innumerable
children's books, nature memoirs, hunting accounts and frontier
histories. Raccoons have been beloved pets of rich and poor alike,
their distinctive skins and tails have been taken and transformed
into popular clothing and headwear, their flesh has been alternately valued and derided as a source of sustenance. They have
inspired the names of hunts, hounds and housecats, along with a
particularly vicious racist slur. And wherever they live, raccoons
inhabit a curious outlaw status, abiding in the unruly borderlands
of what many humans consider appropriate animal behaviour,
and their seemingly uncanny intelligence, dexterity and determin-
ation make them fascinating and frustrating in equal measure.

As is the case with all real or perceived outlaws, when it comes
to our attitudes towards raccoons, there rarely seems to be a

Common
northern raccoon
(*Procyon lotor*).

7

middle ground: we either love them or hate them. Furtive bandits of the night, ring-tailed raiders of rubbish bins and bird tables, bane of urban homeowners and rural farmers, raccoons are readily associated with lawlessness and uncontrollability. Even their physical characteristics seem designed to polarize: one observer sees adorable impishness in the black facial pelage, banded tail and hunched back, whereas a less generous viewer sees a masked cartoon criminal sneaking around in a striped prison uniform. Further, they seem to be an eerie combination of creatures: sharp-nosed masked faces and inscrutable animal eyes that combine with human-like forepaws, a predilection for 'hand' washing, and an irrepressible intelligence beyond that associated with all but the most 'advanced' primates. They seem predisposed to annoy city and suburban homeowners, showing up unexpectedly to enthusiastically harvest lovingly tended gardens, ravage fish ponds and water features, upend waste containers, loudly mate and den in attics and make a parasite-rich mess with their faeces and food remnants. When confronted, raccoons often seem

Raccoons are unusual among wild animals in being drawn to novelty in their environment rather than being frightened by it. This quality, as much as intelligence and flexibility of habitat and diet, has contributed greatly to their species success in a time of global climate disruption.

WASH YOUR HANDS

Before touching your EYES

DISTRICT OF COLUMBIA SOCIETY FOR THE PREVENTION OF BLINDNESS

The stereotype of the tidy, paw-washing raccoon features in this hand-hygiene health awareness campaign poster, c. 1943.

fearless, even defiant, as if unwilling to concede any ground to our self-proclaimed species superiority.

As raccoon numbers and conflicts with human interests grow, humane raccoon removal and more lethal pest control businesses are flourishing. In 2016 the residents of Toronto, Ontario, which boasts (or bemoans) perhaps the world's largest raccoon population, experienced the seeming failure of their city's $31 million 'raccoon-proof' organic waste green bins shortly after

The raccoon's hunched profile features prominently in one of many animal movement studies from famed nineteenth-century English-American photographer Eadweard Muybridge. Plate 745 of *Animal Locomotion*, 1887, collotype.

introduction. In spite of much-publicized assurances from city officials that the new bins' sophisticated design would thwart raccoon access, complaints rolled in within days. (Contrary to news reports, however, it was brute strength, luck and repetition of success, not clever problem-solving or dextrous use of their digits, that enabled food-motivated raccoons, especially nursing mothers, to pop the lids.[2]) The comments section of nearly every Toronto newspaper and online article then and now includes a litany of anti-raccoon rants and calls for widespread culling, and for every human who delights in the discovery of muddy prints on their front doorstep there are others for whom such signs are an interspecies declaration of war.

Raccoons' behavioural adaptability, unique physiology and insatiable curiosity are keys to their biological success, but these qualities contribute to increasing conflict with their human neighbours, especially as their traditional wild habitations grow more imperilled and cities become more favourable for raccoon expansion. And while the species is more prolific now than at any time

in its evolutionary history, raccoons nevertheless face profound dangers from human love and loathing alike.

Whether in newspaper articles, television documentaries or ostensible natural history, raccoons suffer from a surplus of criminalizing stereotypes and clichés. One can hardly encounter raccoons in the media or popular culture without witnessing

Among the varied collective nouns for raccoons, *gaze* seems particularly appropriate for this uncanny taxidermied trio.

the hackneyed outlaw tropes of raccoons as thieves, robbers, trespassers and vandals. Take this typical headline about a group of raccoons found in an Oregon art gallery: 'Art-loving Criminals: Four Raccoons Caught "Burglarizing" Gallery Go Viral after Cops Post Their Hilariously Incriminating Photo'. In this single story the animals are described variously as 'masked bandits', 'furry fiends', 'invaders' and 'intruders', 'cute crooks', 'bold bandits', 'rascally raccoons' and so on. All this mocking moralizing to describe the natural behaviour of a group of curious raccoons exploring an unusual new habitat.[3]

What happened to the raccoons after their apprehension is unknown, but it is likely that they were euthanized, a frequent

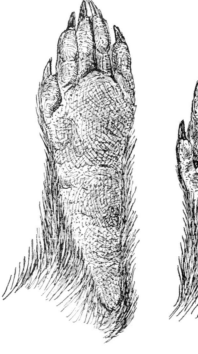

Life study of raccoon hindpaw and forepaw, details from Ernest Thompson Seton's *Life-histories of Northern Animals: An Account of the Mammals of Manitoba* (1909).

There's no hint of the tragedy awaiting many pet raccoons in this early 20th-century scene of a girl and her curious procyonid companion by Missouri photographer Belle Johnson.

end to 'nuisance' animals when authorities are summoned or aggrieved property owners take matters and weapons into their own hands. But dead raccoons are arguably as common in the human imaginary as their living counterparts, abounding in fact and fiction. As fur-bearers, raccoons have played the most significant economic role of any North American fur trade species, and the iconic coonskin has influence well beyond its monetary or fashion value, far surpassing that of the beaver.[4] Just as their skins have long warmed heads and bodies and variously served to represent the American frontier, wilderness masculinity and economic excess, so too do their carcasses serve as symbols of death, natural decay and the afterlife. Dead raccoons are as much disruptive figures as their living counterparts, quite literally embodying some of our deepest existential anxieties about modernity and mortality.

Yet for all their ambivalent associations, raccoons are also respected throughout the world for the same qualities that make them reviled. In a news cycle awash with depressing reports of climate collapse, species extinction and ecological devastation on an incomprehensible scale, the story of the common northern raccoon (*Procyon lotor*) is largely one of successful adaptation to a radically changing planet. Raccoons are increasingly at home in traffic-jammed cities and are among the wild animals most frequently encountered in urban spaces. And as those spaces expand, so too do raccoon populations.

Millions of humans live alongside and encounter raccoons, yet these queer creatures remain largely misunderstood and often despised. When I informed a friend and former neighbour that

Raccoon in Ernest Thompson Seton's animal-focused volume of *The Nature Library* (1926); colour lithograph by McGinn.

I was writing a book on raccoons, she responded with good-natured incredulity: 'Who'd want to read a book about *that*?' As an avid gardener and birder who has experienced years of property destruction by her raccoon neighbours, she is decidedly a partisan of the 'raccoon-as-pest' view, and sees them very differently from the creatures I look upon with curiosity and delight. Same animals, different contexts. This is certainly the case for many species, but raccoons embody these complexities in distinctive ways.

Throughout this book we will consider raccoons as clever, opportunistic animals, living beings with their own sense-worlds, motivations and histories, and as boundary-breaching beasts in human imaginations, customs, relations, ideologies and economies. It is not a comprehensive study, but one that, like raccoons

The raccoon's association with outlawry and disregard for human property is evoked in this wry graffiti wheatpaste of a doubly-masked anarchist raccoon in Berkeley, California, 2012.

themselves, dabbles a bit in and among the representational currents, seeking out meaningful matters to consider more closely. From gun-wielding intergalactic superheroes to despoilers of Japanese Shintō shrines, targets of coon hunts to symbol of racist stereotype, unmanageable pets and neighbourhood nemeses, *Raccoon* cuts a quirky trail through the complex histories and increasingly global impacts of this inquisitive outlaw species.

As we will soon see, this is increasingly the raccoon's world – we just live in it.

1 The Beast Itself: Raccoon Natural History

You may play a trick on a raccoon once, but you will never have the opportunity to repeat your cleverness.
Vance Joseph Hoyt, *Bar-Rac*[1]

The raccoon is the most prominent species among a related group of mammals known to zoologists as the procyonids. In modern scientific nomenclature, the family Procyonidae includes six genera and up to eighteen different species. With the exception of those raccoon populations deliberately or accidentally introduced into places like Germany, Japan and Russia, and those animals living as pets or in fur farms and zoos throughout the world, modern procyonids are exclusive to the Americas. (The red panda of the Himalayas and China was long considered a near relative, but it is now categorized as the sole surviving member of the more distant family Ailuridae and is therefore excluded from this discussion.) Based on current scientific consensus, Procyonidae includes raccoons, ringtails, cacomistles, coatis, olingos, kinkajous and the recently identified olinguitos.

Procyonids share a few common features. They are small- to medium-sized mammals of the order Carnivora, inhabiting the ecological mesopredator niche between apex carnivores and smaller prey species. They evolved for climbing the trees that are still their preferred habitat feature, and all have dextrous paws with bare soles and curved claws to help them navigate tree branches, flexible ankle joints for climbing and descending, and prominent tails that in part help with balance in the canopy. They have large, dark eyes, roundish ears and long, broad bodies. They are generally gender dimorphic, with males larger and heavier than females; couplings are typically promiscuous and temporary, and females generally raise the young alone. Most procyonids are nocturnal and omnivorous, although food availability may shift activity patterns, especially those of the opportunistic raccoon. While mostly solitary aside from mating season, procyonid social structures vary, from territorial kinkajou loners to communal coati matriarchies. The males of most procyonids are known in English as boars, the females sows, and the young either kits, cubs or pups.

Procyonids enter the fossil record in what is now northern Europe and Asia during the Oligocene epoch, about 30 million years ago, making their way to North America roughly 10 million years later during the Miocene. Asserting firm claims about their evolutionary history is complicated by a relative lack of fossils, and their origins and relationships with other species have long been matters of debate and uncertainty. Yet observers have long noted unmistakable similarities between raccoons and the more familiar and widely distributed bears and dogs. Raccoon

Although raccoons have adapted well to urban attics, derelict buildings and other human architecture, they evolved for arboreal living, and trees and wooded areas remain their favoured habitat.

Due to a variety of physical similarities, scientists long classified the red panda (top) among the procyonids, although it is now widely recognized as belonging to a related family of its own. Colour plate from Hugh Craig's 1897 *The Animal Kingdom*.

is a younger sibling to Bear in some Indigenous traditions; in a Nimiipuu story a raccoon grandmother transforms into a grizzly bear after cloaking herself in a dead bear's skin; among the Shawnee people, Raccoon and Bear are associated in both clan roles and ceremony. Similarly, the eighteenth-century founder of modern biological taxonomy, Carl Linnaeus, identified raccoons among the Ursidae – the bears – in both the 1740 and 1758 editions of his great categorizing work, *Systema naturae*. Initially he designated raccoons *Ursus cauda elongata* ('bear with long tail'), but by 1758 settled instead on *Ursus lotor* ('washer bear'), with the latter referring to the animal's supposed habit of cleaning its food with its forepaws.[2]

It was, however, the German naturalist Gottlieb Conrad Christian Storr who in 1780 distinguished raccoons from bears under their own genus, *Procyon*, a nod to their association with dogs. (Storr also gave the scientific name to the raccoon's procyonid relative, the coati.) While Storr disagreed with the *Ursus*

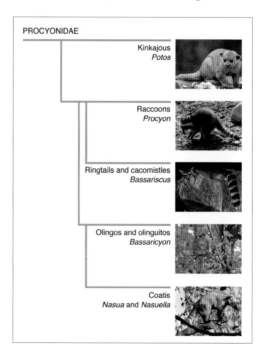

PROCYONIDAE

Kinkajous
Potos

Raccoons
Procyon

Ringtails and cacomistles
Bassariscus

Olingos and olinguitos
Bassaricyon

Coatis
Nasua and *Nasuella*

Evolutionary cladogram of family Procyonidae by Derek Tan. This visual representation of ancestral kinship highlights the shared features of this diverse arboreal family.

association, *lotor* remained as the holdover from Linnaeus's earlier categorization. In Linnaeus's Swedish, the raccoon is known as *tvättbjörn*, or 'washer bear'; Storr's German *Waschbär* translates as the same. So whether it was related to bears or dogs, both men could agree that this creature was a washer, and thus

Procyonids confounded European observers for centuries, and misattribution in Enlightenment-era scientific treatises and natural history texts is not uncommon. This supposed raccoon in the German edition of Conrad Gesner's *Historia animalium* (1563) seems rather to be a South American coati (*Nasua nasua*).

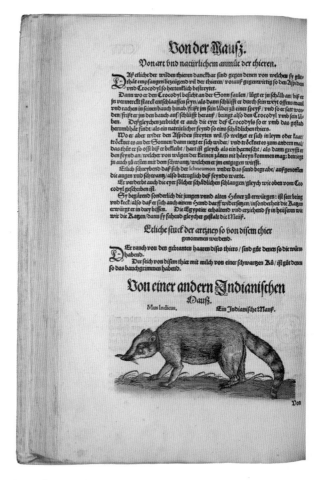

the early *Ursus lotor* became the more familiar *Procyon lotor* and has remained such among scientists for over two hundred years.

Yet dog associations are not uncommon; naturalist Virginia C. Holmgren identifies seven different Indigenous names for raccoons that refer to their doglike qualities. She also posits that the creatures identified by Christopher Columbus as *perro mastin* – 'clownlike dog' – from his first invasion expedition were, in fact, raccoons.[3] Storr's choice of *Procyon* for the raccoon's Latin name was therefore part of a longer history of association drawing from diverse sources. According to zoologist Samuel I. Zeveloff,

> *Procyon* is a Latin term meaning 'before the dog' or 'early dog.' Why Storr selected this term is not known, though it is highly unlikely that he thought of raccoons as being ancestral to dogs . . . In the previous century, astronomers had also used the name Procyon for a newly discovered binary, or double, star in the constellation Canis Minor, which appears in the heavens shortly before Sirius, the Dog Star.[4]

Whatever Storr's reasoning, raccoons are indeed related to dogs, albeit separated by tens of millions of years. So whether firmly terrestrial or poetically celestial, the association of raccoons with dogs and bears is borne out to some degree in their genes and palaeobiology.

Based on current phylogenetic research and the relatively sparse fossil record, and acknowledging the ongoing debate on dates and ancestral relationships, the best guess we have right now is that procyonids' closest relatives are to be found among the weasel-kin of family Mustelidae. Around 40–50 million years ago, the dog-like carnivores of suborder Caniformia began to split into two main branches: the immediate ancestors of dogs and other canids (Canidae) and those of infraorder Arctoidea – which includes today's bears (Ursidae), true seals, fur or eared seals, sea lions and walruses (Pinnipedia) – and those of superfamily Musteloidea, which includes red pandas (Ailuridae) and skunks (Mephitidae), along with Mustelidae and Procyonidae. Today's raccoons share a common ancestry with weasels, badgers, martens, wolverines and other mustelids dating back around 30–35 million years, making them nearer kin compared to those of Canidae and Ursidae, though still distant.

Moving closer in time to roughly 20 million years ago – from the late Miocene into the late Pliocene – the six living procyonid genera evolved from their musteloid ancestors in the jungles of what is now Central America and the southernmost part of North America. Olingos, olinguitos and especially kinkajous are more

Etching of a common raccoon and North American badger (*Taxidea taxus*) from John D. Godman's *American Natural History* (*c.* 1826).

exclusively tree-dwelling fruit eaters, whereas the more omnivorous raccoons, coatis, ringtails and cacomistles are at ease foraging on the ground, higher in the canopy or on rocky outcroppings.

From their Central American origins the various procyonids spread out during a period known as the Great American Biotic Interchange, a series of 'dispersal events' of plants and animals between North and South America made possible when the Panamanian Isthmus rose up around 2.5 million years ago to bridge the previously separated continents. Many species – including early raccoons – began to expand widely across the now-linked Americas.[5] Current phylogenetic analysis of procyonids indicates that raccoons, ringtails and cacomistles comprise one clade (a grouping of species descended from a common ancestor), with coatis, olingos and olinguitos similarly related, and kinkajous a distinctive taxus within the larger Procyonidae family.[6] Kinkajous diverged earliest from the common ancestor – roughly 22 million years ago – whereas the split between the coati/olingo clade and the raccoon/ringtail/cacomistle clade happened somewhere around 18–20 million years ago, with further species delineation taking place in the last 2 million years or so.

In the aftermath of the Great American Biotic Interchange, coatis remained largely tropical, establishing themselves in what is currently Central America, Mexico and the extreme southern United States, or migrating into South America with the olingos, olinguitos and kinkajous. The ringtails and cacomistles would claim the more arid geography of today's central to northern Mexico and the southwestern and central plateau regions of the United States. Most of the 25 common raccoon subspecies are found north of Mexico; except for localized subspecies on some coastal islands and throughout Central America, and the almost entirely South American species, the crab-eating raccoon (*Procyon cancrivorus*), they moved to the more seasonally variable regions of today's continental U.S. and southern Canada. All procyonids would survive upheavals in climate and geography during the Pleistocene epoch and into our own Holocene. It is in this latter period that *Homo sapiens* emerged to dominate the planet and radically alter procyonid fortunes.

Many scientists today argue that our current era is best understood as the Anthropocene, an epoch of massive global human impact – almost entirely a result of capitalist industrialization, corporate resource extraction and petro-pollution – on both the Earth's geology and its lifeforms, with consequences including estimated planetary species loss of over 60 per cent since 1970 alone.[7] Most procyonid populations today are in identifiable decline due to deforestation and habitat degradation, especially the more strictly arboreal olingos and kinkajous. While little is known even now about the status of ringtails, cacomistles and olinguitos, their increasingly diminishing habitats and more specialized reproductive and feeding behaviours leave little room for long-term optimism if current trends continue. On the whole, the industrial Anthropocene has not been kind to procyonids.

Yet for the common northern raccoon the story is very different, as it joins the similarly generalist coyotes and crows as being among the few wild animals worldwide actually *increasing* as a result of human activity, especially in urban areas. Listed by the International Union for Conservation of Nature (IUCN) Red List as being a species of 'least concern', raccoons are now widely distributed throughout North America, and with climate change rendering northern latitudes more temperate, their range is dramatically expanding.[8] Introduced globally for fur farming, the pet trade or zoo exhibition, many raccoons escaped or were intentionally released; with little competition or apex predator threats, the result has generally been explosive population growth. There are more raccoons alive in the world today over a

The Beaver *p.176*

The Racoon *p.182*

p.183
The Brown Coati

The Black Coati
p.183
Ditto

Raccoon among coatis and a beaver, from an abridged London edition of the Comte de Buffon's *Natural History* (*Histoire naturelle*); copper plate engraving, 1792.

larger, transcontinental geographic range than ever before. This is a remarkable story, but all the more so because their population nadir, as best can be determined, was less than a century ago, largely due to commercial demand for their fur.

Raccoons are not the most agile tree climbers in the animal kingdom – kinkajous are far better, as are monkeys and even common tree squirrels. They are not the most social of the procyonids – that distinction goes to coatis. They are good but not exceptional swimmers, lingering mostly at the water's edges. They have neither the most luxuriant fur, the most dramatic markings, nor the loudest, most variable or most melodious calls. Yet it is their generalist nature, not specificity, and a distinctive combination of otherwise commonplace attributes such as intelligence, agility, adaptation, opportunism and flexible omnivorism that

The iconic mask of the common northern raccoon depends as much on the white boundary fur on its muzzle, forehead and cheeks as the black hair around its eyes.

have most contributed to the raccoon's success as a species in spite of human exploitation and aggression.

And while today they are well known through popular culture, film and literature, and although long familiar to Indigenous peoples in the Americas as other-than-human kin, neighbours and ceremonial figures as well as source of food, fur and fun, there was a time when raccoons were exotic creatures to much of the world. The curious range of collective nouns for raccoons – gaze, nursery or mask – indicate something of this strangeness.[9] Raccoons confounded their European observers, for their features and habits seemed to resemble a hybrid host of more familiar animals, and a classification system that associated type with biological similarity was ill-suited to accommodate such seemingly anomalous beasts. In *The Hunter's Feast; or, Conversations around the Camp-fire* (1855), Captain Mayne Reid quoted this imaginative but not inaccurate description of a raccoon: 'the limbs of a bear, and the body of a badger, the head of a fox, the nose of a dog, the tail of a cat, and sharp claws, by which it climbs trees like a monkey'.[10] It seems a good synthesis of the various species proposed as the raccoon's taxonomic near-kin. (Reid did, however, dispute the cat tail comparison; he praised the raccoon's own 'full and bushy' tail as one of its 'chief beauties'.)

Were raccoons a sort of strange tree-dwelling cat, as indicated by *chat sauvage* (wildcat), or even a rodent, as per *raton laveur* (washing rat), occasionally interchangeable names given by seventeenth-century French Jesuits and their *voyageur* successors in what would be called Canada? Jesuit missionary Louis Jordan gave three names for the creature he illustrated in the *Codex Canadensis*, his expansive zoological and botanical treatise, compiled around 1700 but unpublished until 1930: 'esseban ou attiron ou chat sauvage', with *esseban* (esiban) and *attiron* (atí:ron) Jordan's attempts to transcribe the respective Anishinaabe and

Raton laveur – 'washing rat' – in Charles Dessalines d'Orbigny's *Dictionnaire universel d'histoire naturelle*, vol. I; hand-coloured steel engraving by Annedouche after an illustration by Edouard Travies, 1849.

Mohawk names for the species.[11] Lake Erie is named for the Erie people, who were also known to the Jesuits as *Nation du Chat* – Cat Nation – but a far more plausible translation is Raccoon Nation given the animal's clear cultural and economic significance, its associations with the local Indigenous nations and the uncertainty of the French translation. Even in Jordan's manuscript there is confusion, as the text accompanying his drawing clearly conflates raccoons with the short-tailed Canadian lynx, and the drawing itself seems to represent an incongruous hybrid of the two tree-climbing species. While at best an ambivalent reference, *chat sauvage* is still most likely a reference to raccoons.

Were these animals a kind of monkey or badger, as some Spanish commentators mused, or a fox, squirrel or badger variant, as some English observers posited?[12] As will be discussed in Chapter Two, the name 'raccoon' comes to English directly from the writings of Captain John Smith, the colonial Virginia Company entrepreneur famed for his much-exaggerated association with Pocahontas. Various colonial observers returned home with

Taxonomical uncertainty in the 17th-century *Codex Canadensis*: the French missionary term *chat sauvage* – wildcat – was listed alongside the Anishinaabe *esiban* and Mohawk *atí:ron* for raccoon (lower left).

anecdotes of these strange beasts and tried, to varying degrees of success, to accurately describe them to a European audience with no domestic counterpart.

One of the best such descriptions comes from Mark Catesby's 1731 *The Natural History of Carolina, Florida and the Bahama Islands,* the first fully illustrated and published study of North American beasts and botanicals, which fuelled interest in the natural history of the so-called 'New World'. Catesby was writing for an audience largely unfamiliar with many of the creatures he chronicled, and his descriptions remain compelling in their clarity and curiosity. Pre-Linnaeus, the English Catesby identified the raccoon taxonomically as *Vulpi affinis Americana* –roughly translated, 'American fox-kin' – and offers his readers what remains a helpful summary:

> The Raccoon is somewhat smaller, and has shorter Legs than a Fox, it has short pointed Ears, a sharp Nose, and a Brush Tail, transversely marked with black and gray, the Body is gray, with some black on its Face and Ears. They resemble a Fox more than any other Creature, both in Shape and Subtlety, but differ from him in their Manner of Feeding, which is like that of a Squirrel, and in not

While the stereotypical raccoon pelage is grizzled grey, there is considerable diversity in fur colour. Variants like this blonde raccoon are not unknown; Newcastle Island and the Sunshine Coast in British Columbia both have blonde raccoon populations.

burrowing in the Ground; they are numerous in *Virginia* and *Carolina*, and in all the Northern Parts of *America*, and a great Nuisance to Corn Fields and Henroosts; their Food is also Berries, and all other wild Fruit. Near the Sea, and large Rivers, Oysters and Crabs are what they very much subsist on; they disable Oysters when open, but thrusting in one of their Paws, but are often catch'd by the sudden closing of it, and so fast (the Oyster being immoveably [*sic*] fixed to a Rock of others) that when the Tide comes in they are drowned. They lie all the Day in hollow Trees, and dark shady *Swamps*: At Nights they rove about the Woods for Prey; their Flesh is esteemed good Meat, except when they eat Fish.[13]

This description is largely accurate, although the 'raccoon-trapping oyster' story was an unsubstantiated trope even by Catesby's time, and his alternately admiring and bemused description of behaviour, habitat, diet, personality and folklore has the ring of familiarity to contemporary readers who live among raccoons.

Catesby describes the raccoons of Virginia and South Carolina with which he was immediately familiar. Yet of all the procyonids, raccoons show the most variability in size and appearance among three distinct raccoon species and over twenty subspecies, from slender, roundish-faced and short-furred raccoons of coastal Mexico, Central America and South America, to bulkier, darker and more imposing raccoons moving northward towards the boreal forests of Canada – a textbook example of Bergmann's rule, wherein animals with wide geographic distribution are larger in higher latitudes than their counterparts approaching the equator. Along with size, raccoon fur density increases with latitude, and the raccoons most familiar in popular culture are those

This reddish raccoon sports a more unusual fur colour.

of the eastern and northeastern parts of the u.s. and southeastern Canada, with white paw hair and thicker, more grizzled grey-brown pelage than that of their warm-weather relatives. The common northern raccoon's tail aids in balance and provides vital fat storage, especially for those animals in colder habitats with winter scarcity; it is about half the animal's body length among northern raccoons, smaller in length but wider and thicker comparatively than those of its more southerly and tropical counterparts, whose thinner tails average about two-thirds the length of their head and body.

Aside from the common northern raccoon (*Procyon lotor*), there are two other raccoon species. The critically endangered pygmy raccoon (*Procyon pygmaeus*) of Cozumel in Mexico is aptly named, as it is smaller than other species at roughly 3–3.5 kg (6.5–7.8 lb) for both sexes. The crab-eating raccoon (*Procyon cancrivorus*) is nearly as widespread in South America as *Procyon lotor* is in North America, and its four subspecies are more catlike in appearance than their foxish northern cousins, with long, dark-furred legs and a shorter muzzle, ears and coat; it is the largest species overall, averaging 55–75 cm (22–30 in.) (with the bold banded tail adding another two-thirds in length) and 3–8 kg (6.5–17.5 lb). Yet the northern raccoon actually has the greatest weight range, from a low of 2–7 kg (4–15 lb) for females and

The South American crab-eating raccoon is distinguished from its northern relative by its shorter muzzle, longer legs and less dense hair, as shown in this illustration from Buffon's encyclopaedic 18th-century masterwork. Hand-painted engraving by O. de Vries from Jacques de Sève's original illustration.

2–11 kg (4–24 lb) for males all the way up to a massive 10 kg (22 lb) and 28 kg (62 lb) respectively.[14] (These are weights from the wild. The heaviest raccoon on record was a domesticated northern raccoon named Bandit, who weighed an astonishing 34 kg (75 lb) when he died in Pennsylvania in 2004.[15])

Catesby was insightful about raccoon habitat and feeding behaviour. Like other procyonids, raccoons prefer areas with substantial tree cover, especially those with a predictable water source, either natural or human-made; their association with swamp and marsh habitats contributed to negative colonial attitudes towards the species. The protective cover is important – while adaptive to most environments, and not averse to taking over other animals' earth dens, raccoons tend to avoid exposed areas like grasslands and deserts unless human-made constructions are available, whether inhabited or abandoned. Even in cities they tend to prefer treed areas with water and thus more abundant food sources nearby, with a marked preference for neglected or relatively unmonitored edge regions and fencerows, which can

Although better known for their tree-climbing abilities, raccoons are capable swimmers and comfortable enough with long periods afloat to ably defend themselves in the water from wild predators or hunting hounds.

36

The cuteness, curiosity and vulnerability of raccoon kits belie the physically and intellectually formidable adults they will become.

be primary habitat or merely transmission corridors between areas of abundance and protection.[16] That raccoons flourish on the boundary between the wild and the cultivated reflects their consistent symbolic representation as existing in the extralegal borderlands between order and chaos.

Habitat determines diet, but there is almost no food source that the omnivorous raccoons will not exploit, and they can easily subsist on a varied range from molluscs, crustaceans, fish, nesting birds and their eggs, small mammals, reptiles, amphibians and invertebrates, to all manner of fruits, nuts, tubers and other edible plants – to say nothing of human crops, garden plants, pet food and random food waste in compost bins, rubbish containers, dumpsters and landfills. The clash between agriculturalists and raccoons has a long history: among Mayan farmers in the Classic Period (roughly 250–950 CE) the raccoon and its coati cousin were decried as cornfield raiders while also associated with a bountiful harvest; the frustration from Catesby's time mirrors that of today's rural farmers and city homeowners, who not infrequently find their long-tended crops, floral displays, garden fish ponds, bird houses and manicured lawns harvested by hungry raccoons, and more than a few urbanites with home chicken coops have found their feathered charges decimated by a midnight raid.[17] Hobby birders and urban conservationists can also be antagonistic to the species for its impact on nest protection efforts for endangered birds and reptiles.

The Scots-Canadian naturalist and nature writer Ernest Thompson Seton (1860–1946) observed that it

> is a common thing to find half-a-dozen Coons in one hollow tree. It is a rare thing to find a solitary Coon. Therefore, I consider the Coon a social animal. But they do not run in bands, except as families, nor are several nests placed together; therefore, they are but slightly gregarious.[18]

Indeed, raccoons can be solitary or social depending on food and territory pressures. Where food resources are abundant you will find greater intraspecies tolerance and even opportunistic co-operation, especially in high-density urban areas, although the sexes tend to group separately except in cases of mothers caring for the current year's young. Multiple den sites across any given territory are the norm.

Raccoons have a diverse range of calls and vocalizations, from hisses and barks to chittering chirrups, revving purrs and almost human screams, the last of which are most common in mating season. Mating is a late winter or early spring affair, depending on the region, with births following two to three months later. Litters range from as few as one to five or more, with kits able to forage independently by around four months of age. Lifespan in the wild is generally between five and ten years; in captivity, it can be twice that.

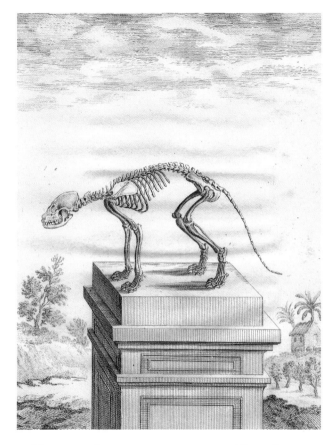

The greatest threats to raccoons are automobile traffic, starvation, parasites and disease rather than predators, with canine distemper and rabies their chief disease afflictions. Distemper poses a particular risk to urban raccoon populations given the higher concentration of animals and the potential for rapid transmission, both among raccoons in close proximity and between raccoons, cats and dogs. Indeed, urban raccoons are so susceptible to this highly contagious disease that an entire community can be nearly wiped out within days by an unchecked distemper outbreak.[19] *Baylisascaris procyonis*, the raccoon roundworm, is a particularly notorious parasite, especially as it is transmissible to humans through disturbed raccoon faeces and has been fatal or permanently debilitating in very rare cases.[20] Raccoons are a vector species for rabies, but are more of a danger to one another and to house pets than to humans.

Human hunting and trapping, while still common, do not seem to have much negative impact on overall raccoon numbers today, although it can decimate local populations. The commercial demand for raccoon skins was at its peak in the nineteenth and the early to mid-twentieth century; nineteenth-century numbers are hard to assess given incomplete data, but at least 13 million raccoon pelts went to England alone from the 1840s to the 1860s.[21] In his 1909 *Life-histories of Northern Animals*, Seton estimated a North American raccoon population of 4 million, indicating a significant drop in numbers from the mid-nineteenth century; he also observed that raccoons had been entirely wiped out of some areas.[22] Since then, human-caused habitat expansion, industrial agriculture and predator extermination have helped

Washbär – 'washing bear' – from Gustav von Hayek's *Grosser Volksatlas der Naturgeschichte aller drei Reiche*, (c. 1885), lithograph.

Waschbär. Procyon lotor. Desm.

RACCOON

Raccoons are featured in Leonard Pearson's *Diseases and Enemies of Poultry* (1897), joining opossums, foxes, bobcats, various raptors and even squirrels on the list of menacing fowl-killers. As the state veterinarian of Pennsylvania, Pearson compiled this two-part compendium in response to legislators' concerns about threats to the state's poultry industry.

raccoon numbers rebound so impressively that the IUCN Red List confidently declares that its current population trend is 'Increasing' with few viable population threats.

Raccoon resurgence and expansion have been facilitated by their aforementioned combination of adaptations for exploiting a wide range of food resources in vertical and horizontal habitats alike, but intelligence deserves ample credit, too. Suzanne MacDonald, an animal behaviourist at York University in Ontario, has studied the species for decades, and points to the raccoon's curiosity as a particularly important contributor to its success:

> Raccoons, if you put something down that they've never seen before, the first thing is to grab it. So they have, instead of this trait to be afraid of things, which is called *neophobia*, which just means 'new phobia', right, they have *neophilia*, which means that they like new things and they will actually approach and investigate new things. They see our garbage cans and they say, great. And they have their little paws and they say, wonderful, thank you, you know? Whereas most species would not approach human structures like that.[23]

In the early twentieth century raccoons were the subject of scientific experimentation and debate, especially in the field of psychology, and some researchers considered them an ideal species for comparative analysis. Much of the debate focused on whether raccoons had actual minds, distinctive personalities and motivations and intelligence or were just advanced and undifferentiated 'stimulus-response machines'.[24] (This was also the key issue in the literary 'nature faker' controversy of the period.) As the historian of science Michael Pettit observes, at the time,

> raccoons belonged neither to the managerial world of the 'psychological factory' nor to the naturalistic field; rather they were organisms that inhabited a borderland between these two different scientific zones . . . The raccoon's existence as an animal of these borderlands made it a captivating object of study and a source of incredulity.[25]

That the raccoon was so clearly liminal here, too, is entirely in keeping with the trend of representations we will see throughout this book.

Yet not all observers have found raccoon cognition or its associated neophilia worthy of praise. Ernest Ingersoll, an early twentieth-century nature writer and contemporary of Seton, was not much impressed with raccoon intellectual capacity, as indicated by this somewhat sniffy observation:

> This simplicity of mind, which makes him unsuspicious of novelties, seems to show that he is not entitled to all of the reputation for acuteness that has been given to him. Perhaps the fox is his superior in real mental capacity, but the raccoon is so far beyond Reynard and many other

highly sagacious beasts in manual dexterity that he *appears* to be quite as clever as the best of them.[26]

Ingersoll was not entirely without regard for the raccoon's abilities, as he firmly dismissed Catesby's folk story of the raccoon held fast in an oyster's grip until the tide came in to drown it: 'the 'coon is not only too quick-witted but too nimble to be caught in a trap acting so slowly as that.'[27]

More recently, researchers have returned to the issue of raccoon intelligence. The 'Aesop's Fable paradigm' was named for Aesop's story 'The Crow and the Pitcher', in which a crow, dying of thirst, finds a pitcher with water at the bottom; unable to reach it, the clever bird drops stones into the pitcher until the water level is high enough to drink. (The phrase 'necessity is the mother of invention' comes from this fable.) Animal cognition researchers have tested this scenario on birds and primates, as well as raccoons, putting cut-up marshmallows at the bottom of a vertical cylinder, and adding enough water to keep the sweets floating

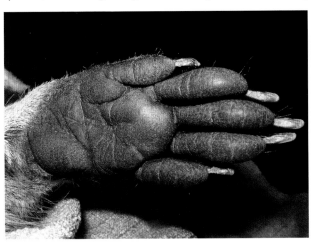

Raccoon forepaws are remarkably dextrous; even without an ape's opposable thumb they have little difficulty with complicated manual tasks such as gaining entry to human dwellings, secured backyard sheds, and chicken coops, as many outraged homeowners and gardeners can attest.

out of reach. Five small stones were then placed on a thick ledge at the top of the tube. There was an even ratio of female to male raccoons, both wild-caught and captive-born. The animals started without training and researchers simply let the raccoons encounter the test directly; later they undertook learning trials. The results were mixed: only two of the eight raccoons succeeded by the end, at least according to the expected research scenarios. A third gave the researchers a surprise: '[she] innovated a unique solution by gripping the inner rim of the apparatus with her forepaws and, while rocking her body back and forth, overturned the entire apparatus and retrieved the reward.'[28] When arbitrary human rules proved an obstacle, manual improvisation and direct force achieved the desired result. (This also seems to be the case with the Toronto green-bin breaches discussed in the Introduction.)

For raccoons, there is an intriguing connection between their intelligence and their famously dextrous forepaws. As we have noted, the second part of their taxonomic name – *lotor* – means 'washer', and their association with washing, scratching, dousing and similar behaviours is reflected in at least two dozen Indigenous and European names for the animals.[29] Their preference for treed habitats with nearby waterways, combined with the widespread observation of dunking crayfish, molluscs and other foods in water before eating, has led to the common belief that raccoons wash their meals.

The truth is far more fascinating. Yes, raccoons often wet and digitally manipulate their food and other objects, but not so much to clean as to *read* them with the sensitive hairless pads of their forepaws. Their paws are not uniquely responsive among mammals to sensory stimuli (our own hands are more acute), but the area of the raccoon brain that interprets such input – the somatosensory cortex of the posterior cerebrum – is comparably larger

Dousing of food and unfamiliar objects is an iconic raccoon behaviour that informs many Indigenous and non-Indigenous names for the species.

than that of other procyonids.[30] This enables them to assess and understand what they are holding more thoroughly than with vision alone, as demonstrated when they manipulate objects with their forepaws while looking elsewhere, thus remaining visually attentive to potential threats. The entire relationship between dousing and forepaw anatomy is still not entirely understood, but it does seem that water helps to heighten the sensitivity of their soft, nerve-rich skin and enables the raccoon to pick up information not otherwise available via sight, smell and taste.

Aside from the forepaws and ringed tails, the most celebrated physical trait of raccoons is their facial mask. Yet it has long been unclear just what purpose it serves. In a 2005 study, biologists Chris Newman, Christina D. Buesching and Jerry O. Wolff tested a series of hypotheses about mask function by comparing the habitats, behaviours and evolutionary histories and biological

Three raccoons of varying pelage shade and pattern share the bold mask and shining eyes for which the species is known worldwide.

niches of various 'midguild' carnivores with distinctive facial markings, including badgers, polecats, civets, skunks, wolverines and raccoons. They determined that of all the hypotheses – preventing sun glare, social identification at a distance, guiding bites away from sensitive eyes, sexual/mate selection, camouflage from prey, and warning to competitors and predators alike – the latter seemed the most reasonable explanation.[31]

Raccoons are certainly well adapted for the diverse environments in which they live, yet it is not only their biology and behaviour that make raccoons a fascinating subject for study. We now turn our attention to the symbolic raccoon–human interface, and the ways they have been represented in our languages, lore and arts, as well as our social relations, economies and daily lives. In many ways, the raccoons of fact are much obscured by the raccoons of fiction. But as we have already seen, raccoons are nothing if not adaptable, and even in their most negative encounters with humans they have, as a species, managed to emerge better than we might have anticipated.

2 Raccoons of Symbol and Story

A keen face, yet very innocent, in which dog intelligence and fox cunning and bear drollery mingled perfectly; a face full of surprises, that set you smiling and thinking at once; a fascinating, inquisitive face, the most lovable and contradictious among the Wood Folk.

William J. Long, *A Little Brother to the Bear*[1]

In the 1930s, looters unearthed a cache of materials from what is today known as the Craig Mound, in the Spiro Mounds cultural heritage site in eastern Oklahoma. Among the plundered objects are two large marine shell engravings dating back perhaps eight hundred years. One is a whelk gorget inscribed with the image of a raccoon skin hanging from a striped post above two dancing human figures. The second is of a great tree surrounded at the base by floating eyes or leaves; on each of its ten symmetrical branches stands a stylized raccoon in profile.

The Spiro site is one of the most significant locales belonging to what scholars today call the 'Mississippian Ideological Interaction Sphere' or the 'Southeastern Ceremonial Complex', a widespread artistic, ceremonial, iconographic, culture and trade economy that extended from the upper Mississippi River region to the edge of the Great Plains through what is now much of the American Southeast all the way to the Gulf of Mexico. Although the timeline had regional variations, the full flowering of Mississippian culture lasted from roughly 900 CE to the early eighteenth century, when extended conflicts with French forces led survivors of the great Natchez chiefdom to find refuge among their kin and neighbours in the Southeast. Mississippian iconography continues to influence contemporary Indigenous artists descended from these diverse but interconnected peoples.

A juvenile raccoon watches observers with mingled curiosity and caution.

49

The specific symbolism of the Spiro Mounds 'Raccoon Priests Shell Gorget' remains unclear, but between this raccoon-adorned neckpiece and other objects from this and related sites there is ample evidence that raccoons were ceremonially significant to Indigenous peoples of what is now the southeastern U.S. during the Mississippian period.

At its height the Mississippian tradition was marked by astronomically oriented earthen mound complexes, extensive maize cultivation, ritual warfare with centralized power and urbanization under increasingly influential chiefdoms, and a roughly shared cosmology of upper, middle and lower worlds connected by a sacred pillar, tree or mountain. This three-tiered cosmos was inhabited by powerful spirit beings that combined human and animal qualities, including those of the raccoon (whose prominent eye mask and banded tail are well represented in Mississippian symbolism).

With the exception of carved stone pipe bowls that predate the Mississippian period by a few hundred years, the Craig Mound gorget and raccoon tree carving offer the most striking raccoon images produced in these regions. The 'Raccoon Priests Shell Gorget' features two human figures dancing back to back, arms aloft with rattle or club in hand, each wearing a skirt of raccoon skins with banded tails dangling. They dance around a striped pole, likely representing the great tree linking the Above and Below Worlds, from which hangs the prominently carved raccoon, its masked features facing the viewer, its own tail hanging directly above the centre spiral.

Very different but no less striking are the enigmatic figures on the more stylized 'Tree of Life with Raccoons'. Each raccoon stands at the end of its respective branch looking outward; the tree trunk is marked by bands resembling those on the animals' tails. Their masks are clearly defined, with eyes mirroring those of the leaf/eyes floating below, but their muzzles are closer to birds' beaks, thus hinting at their arboreal origins and their kinship with the sky as much as the earth.

In Mississippian traditions, the ordered and airy Above World and the chaotic and watery Below World – along with their respective denizens – were in a state of constant struggle. There were firm boundaries between all orders in the terrestrial Between World that humans inhabited in their attempts to find a place of purity and balance between all creation. Adherence to the distinctions between worlds was a major emphasis of Mississippian cosmologies, but there were also powerful entities who breached these boundaries and could move between worlds and their structural categories. These anomalous beings were recognized as possessing powers that were often respected and sometimes feared. Many of these were entirely natural animals that crossed and combined these perceived categories. For example, in Cherokee tradition, while the bat and flying squirrel share many features of terrestrial mammals, both also have the bird's power of flight, and they therefore inhabit an anomalous status between the Above and Between Worlds.[2]

It is no exaggeration to observe that anomaly has long been *the* defining symbolic feature of the potent outlaw raccoon.[3] Their black facial mask is shared with other powerful animals in Southeastern cosmologies, such as the eastern rattlesnake, pileated woodpecker and the peregrine falcon, indicating what is likely a ritual kinship. Their seeming hybridization of other creatures and worlds made them distinctive among their Mississippian neighbours and later observers; their neophilic curiosity would have

The Spiro Mounds gorget features in 'Hasinai Twins', a contemporary piece by the celebrated Caddo Nation potter Jereldine Redcorn.

similarly emphasized their behavioural distinction from most other animals, which, being neophobic, actively avoid us. Given the willingness of raccoons in our own time to take advantage of the resources available in concentrated human populations, it is reasonable to assume that they would have found the increasing urbanization of the Mississippian chiefdoms no less appealing, thereby breaching another categorical boundary between wild and cultivated. And while largely tree dwellers, they spend much of their time hunting and exploring on the ground and even go to water to hunt and examine their food, thus explicitly combining the airy Above, earthy Between and watery Below worlds. What more appropriately powerful anomalous animal than the arboreal/terrestrial/aquatic raccoon, which embodies qualities of them all? This prominent raccoon symbolism is found well beyond Spiro; similar works have been unearthed at another Mississippian site, the Etowah Mounds in current-day Georgia, nearly 1,100 km (685 mi.) away.[4]

Scholars, artists and ceremonialists offer diverse perspectives on the meanings of the raccoon in much of the iconography emerging from the Mississippian Ideological Interaction Sphere. And as very different raccoon-themed art from across the Americas demonstrates, the animals would continue to be significant to Native peoples well beyond that period and that region, and remain so today. Yet the idea of anomaly, like the figure of the outlaw, gives us much to consider, as raccoons have long been seen as category-defying, rule-breaking and boundary-breaching beings in Indigenous traditions throughout the Americas. These associations continue to inform contemporary representations of raccoons around the world.

Even the species' common name is anomalous. Of all the names that might have become familiar to a global audience, 'raccoon' is one of the least likely. It is derived from *arakun* or

Stone raccoon effigy pipe from the Tremper Mound in current-day Ohio. The pipe dates to the Hopewell period, roughly 100 BCE to 400 CE, pre-dating the rise of the Mississippians by about five hundred years.

arakunem, likely an approximation of 'it scratches with its hands', from the related tongues of the Powhatan Confederacy in what is currently called Virginia. Powhatan is one of many affiliated languages within the larger Algonquian language family, but historically it was a relatively localized one; far more common than anything resembling *arakun* across upper and northeastern North America is the Anishinaabe word *esiban*, for 'it picks up things', versions of which are found in other Algonquian languages of at least a dozen more cultural groups, including Cree, Potawatomi, Abenaki and Lenape peoples.

As noted in Chapter One, it is colonialism that brought 'raccoon' into English, and it starts with one of the foundational figures of British colonial expansion in North America: Captain John Smith, who would later be made famous through his heavily fictionalized association with the young Powhatan woman Matoaka (or Amonute), better known in our own time and to his English contemporaries as Pocahontas. Smith was a notorious self-promoter as well as an entrepreneur and leader of the Jamestown settlement, the first of England's permanent colonial enterprises in the Americas. James Fort (later Jamestown) had been erected within Tsenacommacah, the territory controlled by the mighty Powhatan alliance and its influential leader, Wahunsenecawh, or Chief Powhatan. Relations and communications between the Powhatan people and the English invaders were challenging from the beginning and deteriorated quickly, and the enterprise was weakened by internal strife, conflict with Powhatan forces and spiralling death rates due to starvation and disease.

A selection of Indigenous and European names for raccoons across multiple language families in North America. Map by Maya Daurio.

In 1608, responding to increasing scepticism in England about the settlement's survival prospects, Smith anonymously published *A true relation of such occurrences and accidents of noate as hath happened in Virginia . . .*, adding his name to the document only in 1615 after the Jamestown settlement began to see success. It is in this document that Smith tells of meeting 'Emperor' Wahunsenecawh, the latter 'proudly lying vppon a Bedftead a foote high vpon tenne or twelue Mattes, richly hung with manie Chaynes of great Pearles about his necke, and couered with a great Couering of *Rahaughcums*' (emphasis added). Here, then, is our first record of a version of *arakun* in English. In 1612 Smith would offer a different phonetic spelling of the same word: '*There is a beast they call Aroughcun, much like a badger*, but vseth to live on trees as Squirrels doe' (italics in original).[5] About twenty years later, William Woods offered the clipped *Rackoone* in his *New England's Prospect*, and 'raccoon' would quickly become what we recognize as the standard English form of the word.

Of course, there are many Indigenous names for the animal today known worldwide as raccoon, and most of these names are still very much alive, as are the languages and traditions in which they feature. To add just a few examples to those above, among some of the Mississippian-connected cultures from the u.s. Southeast, names range from my own Cherokee Nation's *kvhli* or *kvtli* in the Overhill Cherokee dialect of what is now Oklahoma, to *wó:tko* in the language of our Muscogee (Creek) neighbours, where the clan named for the animal is *wo:tk-âlki*. Insomnia and mourning are said to be Wó:tko's doing, for he is 'always roaming around at night and grieving, as is shown by the white circles around his eyes'.[6] The Chickasaws, like the Muscogees, also have a prominent Raccoon Clan (*Iksa' Shawi'*), whereas among their immediate relatives, the Choctaw people, the Raccoon Dance continues to be an important cultural practice. (The Louisiana

Cajun word for raccoon, *chaoui*, gestures to the French Canadian *chat sauvage* but is more certainly derived from their Chickasaw and Choctaw neighbours, whose words for the animal – *shawi'* and *shaui* respectively – mean something like 'grasper'.[7])

In her wide-ranging *Raccoons in History, Folklore and Today's Backyards*, Virginia C. Holmgren includes dozens of Indigenous terms for raccoons and categorizes them according to shared themes, such as 'names describing agile forepaws' (with the Algonquian *arakun* and variants of *esiban* among them), 'names describing face', 'names implying magic', 'names describing big tail', 'names comparing to dog', 'names indicating eaters of crabs, crayfish' and so on.[8] While not all her offered definitions can be easily tracked or confirmed and some seem to draw on unreliable or dated sources, the list remains a useful starting point for considering not just the diversity of names and understandings for this animal, but also the continuities between naming conventions and cultural curiosity expressed across geographical distance.

Of course, terminology is just one way to articulate meaningful relations – story is another. While less prominent than other trickster-transformers like Coyote, Raven and even Rabbit, Raccoon holds a significant place in many Indigenous traditions throughout its wide range. Often rendered as male in these stories (but sometimes changing species and gender along the way), Raccoon is frequently a companion to or foil for other animals and powerful spiritual beings. The tales can be humorous or wondrous, but they can also be quite grim; his now-iconic features are sometimes the result of accidents related to his curiosity or, just as often, punishments for misdeeds such as greed, gluttony and cruelty.

For example, in a Cherokee story Raccoon – Kvhli – is among the more helpful of the animals. In the beginning times, there was no fire, and the People were huddled in cold darkness. Lightning struck a dead tree on an island far from shore, but the People could not reach it, so the animals and birds tried to bring it to them. Kvhli made his way to the island and looked into the hollow tree, but 'the fire flared up and the smoke covered his face and turned it black'; he tried to drop his tail into the hole to get the fire, but parts of it, too, were charred black. Cherokee traditionalist Hastings Shade offers this assessment: 'Today, when you see him you can see he still has a mask on and you can see the rings around his tail . . . He got these things by trying to help the people get the fire.'[9]

Rather than a mark of honour, the mask is sometimes seen as a badge of shame: in one Anishinaabe account, after Esiban mistreats a couple of blind elders under the protection of the culture hero Nanabush (or Nanabozho), the latter punishes him by painting his face black as a public reminder of his unkindness; the celebrated Woodlands-style Odawa artist Daphne Odjig (1919–2016) memorialized this story in her painting *Nanabush Giving the Raccoon Its Colours* (1969) and a later children's book. Yet in a different Anishinaabe story it is the paw-washing Esiban who

Although raccoons are most extensively chronicled in the eastern regions of North America, their territories do stretch throughout the western half of the continent. This *c.* 1899 photograph features a Havasu Baaja (Havasupai) youth with pet raccoon in the Grand Canyon region of current-day Arizona.

teaches personal hygiene to Nanabush, who in turns passes those teachings to humanity.[10]

There is an old Abenaki story of a hungry but lazy Azban play-ing dead in order to deceive a group of crayfish into leaving the safety of a fast-moving stream to come within his easy reach. In a Choctaw account, an envious Possum asks Raccoon how the latter achieved such lovely black rings on his tail; Raccoon shares a complex process of wrapping the tail in vines and lightly singeing the exposed hair in a fire, but neglects to say how long the process should take. The vain and foolish Possum lingers too long and burns away all the hair, and his descendants now have hairless tails as a consequence.[11] Espons loses hair from his own hindquarters in a Passamaquoddy story when, in retribution for viciousness to smaller and weaker animals, he is tricked into eating rose hips that cause him uncontrollable anal itching; he desperately rubs the hair away, and today's raccoons retain that feature.[12]

Most of the stories in *Tales of the Bark Lodges* by Oklahoma Wyendot writer Bertrand N. O. Walker are about Ol' Coon and his various playful scrapes among his animal kin, especially against his sometime nemesis Ol' Fox. Here again he is an anomalous, border-walking figure – wiser than most of his neighbours, but sometimes caught off guard by his own hubris. Walker's animal tales are part of a larger literary tradition of the Indian Territory during the late nineteenth and early twentieth centuries in which Native commentators published in regional and cultural dialect to comment on political issues of the time, through a deliberately exaggerated fictive persona. In the book Ol' Coon is firmly rooted in Indigenous contexts, as the frame narrative is that of a young Wyandot boy listening to stories from his aunt. But in spite of the book's clear anti-Blackness, Walker was also explicitly echoing Joel Chandler Harris's popular Uncle Remus stories and highlighting the narrative links between Black and Indigenous story traditions, with Ol' Coon the Wyendot counterpart to Bre'r Rabbit. (Bre'r Coon was indeed a minor character in Chandler's own stories and the African American story traditions he appropriated, but Bre'r Rabbit was the star of that show.)

Closer to our own time, Drew Hayden Taylor's *Motorcycles and Sweetgrass* (2010) invokes the Anishinaabe tale of Nanabush and the raccoon, but as a kind of mock epic. Taylor, an Ojibway writer from Ontario, imagines the relationship between the trickster-transformer and raccoons as an ongoing war of attrition, one given renewed life when Nanabush rides his motorcycle into the modern reserve community of Otter Lake and discovers hundreds of raccoons waiting for him. While the original Anishinaabe story is one of a raccoon being punished by Nanabush for its mischievous cruelty to a couple of blind men, here it is Nanabush who has erred, having long ago killed and eaten a raccoon who had sought shelter in his camp during a fierce storm. For that act of inhospitality, Nanabush has earned the enmity of subsequent generations of raccoons, from the time of old stories to today, and they are ready for their revenge. In the form of a white man named John Smith (a sly raccoonish reference), Nanabush comes to the community and begins to romance the chief, Maggie Second, who is in complex land repatriation negotiations with the province. This place is special to Nanabush, who has been reduced over the years by the fading memory of his significance among his people; here he is remembered, by humans and raccoons alike.

As an inherently disruptive being, he cannot help but create chaos in Maggie's life and that of the community. But as befits a largely benevolent figure, things come around in a good way by the end as the burdens of the past are dealt with, and new and better relations put in place. This includes Nanabush's long feud with the raccoons, which ends when he finally offers compensation and apology for his ancient act of cruelty. The raccoons return to the woods, and the ever-restless but wiser Nanabush continues on his adventures in the world. Yet there is a shadow, for we know that Maggie's community will continue to deal with colonialism; we know that Nanabush, for all his new-found wisdom, is still largely driven by appetite. Things are better, but much depends on future actions, and raccoons, as Taylor reminds us, have very long memories.

The examples go on, far more than can be included here. But the abundance of raccoon names, stories, dances, clans, ceremonies and interactions across hundreds of nations and languages indicates a long and diverse relational history, one that has only become more complex over time. From early Mississippian arts to contemporary oral, ceremonial and literary traditions, from raccoons as anomalous beings representing the three realms of existence to figures of didactic teaching and playful humour, wherever Raccoon has been the focus of storied attention, he (more rarely another gender) has been considered uncanny, clever, creative, occasionally malevolent, but always a notable animal neighbour. The qualities we have already come to identify with raccoons – adaptability, dexterity, intelligence and mischief – are also the traits of Raccoon/Esiban/Arakun, and they continue to inform the ways humans live with and imagine the animal.

Benson Bond Moore, *Raccoons*, n.d. (pre-1940), etching on laid paper.

Raccoons had been transplanted to Europe as pets and curiosities as far back as the 15th century, although no self-sustaining populations existed until the twentieth. Flemish artist Pieter Boel painted this oil study of a raccoon from life in the Versailles menagerie of King Louis XIV of France, c. 1669–71.

Less common in the visual arts than their real or represented pelts, living raccoons are mostly found in natural history texts, though occasionally figured in noteworthy paintings and statuary. Sometime between 1669 and 1671 the Flemish painter Pieter Boel painted a raccoon and marmots from living captives in Louis XIV's Paris zoo; he was rare among artists of his era for representing not one but two procyonids, with another painting in the series featuring a coati. Louis XIV's court painter, Charles Le Brun, included a bedraggled raccoon among other mammals in his lush allegorical tapestry *The Months; or, The Royal Houses, October, Palais des Tuileries* (1668–80), but it has none of Boel's realism or charm. One delightfully unexpected raccoon appears in Jean Leon Gerome Ferris's *Her Weight in Gold* (likely painted between 1916 and 1917). The American-born Ferris (1863–1930) was first known for his Orientalist subject-matter but became more famous for his romantic American Colonial Revival subjects. The painting depicts a historical event in eighteenth-century Philadelphia where a young bride is weighed on one half of a large goods scale,

Jean Leon Gerome Ferris's *Her Weight in Gold* (oil on canvas, c. 1916–17) was based in part on the dowry weighing of Sarah Richardson after her 1771 Philadelphia wedding to Nicholas Waln. In this romanticized scene the leashed raccoon hints at the peaceful domestication of wild America through marriage and mercantilism.

while her father adds bags of gold coins from her dowry to the counterbalance platform.[13] Her doting new husband stands at her side; leashed to his right hand is an attentive pet raccoon, its presence seemingly as domesticated and commonplace as that of a companion dog.

Back across the Atlantic, the Animal Wall in Cardiff, Wales, features two raccoons. Built as part of the restoration of Cardiff Castle in the nineteenth century, the Animal Wall is a celebrated architectural feature in the city; while originally outside the castle itself, it was later moved to Bute Park. The jutting merlons on a low, crenelated stone wall are topped by fifteen different animal statues. It is unclear why the sculptor, Alexander Carrick, chose these particular non-native 'exotic' animals from across the

Commonwealth, but the raccoons continue to sit in pride of place among the other beasts on the wall.

Literary raccoons are more common than their counterparts in the visual arts, and we will give attention to a few examples here. Even as prolific a writer and artist as the aforementioned Ernest Thompson Seton gave sparse attention to the raccoon in his dozens of animal-themed works for children and adults. Of those, 'Way-atcha, the Coon-raccoon of Kilder Creek' in *Wild Animal Ways* (1916), is an evocative if heavy-handed read. It begins in Seton's signature sentimental prose:

> Mother Nature, All-mother, maker of the woods, that made and rejected the Bear – too big, the Deer – too obvious and too helpless in snow, the Wolf – too fierce and flesh devouring, not deeming them the spirit of the timberland, and still essayed, till the Coon-Raccoon, the black-masked wanderer of the night and the tall timber, responsive from the workshop, came; and dowered him with the Dryad's gifts, a harmless dweller in the hollow oak, the spirit of the swamps remotest from the plow, the wandering voice that redmen know, that white men hear with superstitious dread.[14]

Seton's imaginative style was widely praised by mainstream readers but excoriated by more 'scientific' naturalists like John Burroughs and Theodore Roosevelt, who dismissed him as one of the 'nature fakers' whose romanticizing anthropomorphism dominated the nature writing scene of the time. Yet florid excesses aside, Seton's work demonstrates keen first-hand observation of raccoon habits and habitat, as well as a deep ethical investment in the well-being of an increasingly imperilled natural world and its inhabitants. (Indeed, it is his understanding of animals as

complex emotional beings, not the mechanistic biologism of his critics, that has best withstood scientific scrutiny over time, especially in the field of ethology.)

More in the 'nature fakers' vein are writers like Arthur Scott Bailey, Thornton W. Burgess and Clara Dillingham Pierson, who offered bland, condescending moralizing for their young readers. The eponymous heroes of Bailey's 1915 *The Tale of Fatty Coon* (one of his 'Sleepy-time Tales') and Burgess's 1918 *The Adventures of Bobby Raccoon* (from his Old Mother West Wind series) are raccoons in name only; their adventures are simple and without substantial danger or consequence, and the natural world is largely benign and characters defined in broad strokes. Pierson's *Among the Night People* (1902) attempts to ease children's bedtime fears by telling stories of the 'hundreds and thousands of tiny out-of-door people' and their lives in the darkness, but ultimately reduces the distinctive animal lives and sense-worlds to banality.[15]

These are just a few of many such writers and works, although one powerful exception is Seton's friend and fellow Canadian writer Charles G. D. Roberts. His 1904 story 'Little People of the Sycamore' is an alternately enchanting and harrowing story of a family of raccoons that begins with closely observed study of the mother raccoon providing for her kits and ends in the horror of a coon hunt where she and all but one of her kits are burned out of the sycamore and killed, with the traumatized survivor taken as a hunter's pet. (The accompanying illustration by famed wildlife artist Charles Livingston Bull features the mother hunting for frogs, and her glowing eyes in the twilight seem almost a spectral portent of the fate to come.)

The fate of the last kit is no real surprise, for the subgenre of raccoon pet memoirs as well as literal raccoon pet-making also grows in popularity from this period. Although raccoon pet stories certainly pre-dated Sterling North's award-winning *Rascal:*

The naturalist and writer Ernest Thompson Seton was also an accomplished visual artist. This scene of a mother raccoon and her kits hunting frogs by moonlight exemplifies his careful attention to anatomical detail as well as his more controversial attraction to romanticized compositions.

A Memoir of a Better Era (1963), few of his predecessors caught the public's imagination as firmly as did his coming-of-age story of himself as a lonely boy who finds friendship and purpose in First World War America when he captures a raccoon kit. It would enjoy further popularity when Walt Disney adapted it for the big screen in 1969, and again in an animated Japanese anime series titled *Araiguma Rasukaru* in 1977.

Rascal merits consideration as a literary text, and one that has ongoing relevance to our concerns, for it had an influence well beyond the u.s. and far past the page. The *Rascal* narrative arc, as with so many tales of raccoon–human relations, is one of innocence lost; North adores 'Rascal' and enjoys many humorous experiences with the raccoon as they mature together, but Rascal's growing destructiveness makes him an increasingly unsuitable pet. Eventually young Sterling accepts that Rascal is a wild animal, travels a far distance from home in his canoe, and releases his four-footed friend into the woods, becoming a sadder but wiser person along the way.

Rascal's 'rewilding' facilitates Sterling's entry into the emotional sacrifices of manhood, and it struck a chord in white readers at a time when many of the established social and political presumptions of white America (the 'better era' gestured to in the book's subtitle) were being questioned. And the protagonist's sacrifice of his much-loved pet to a life in the wild was a point of critical praise.[16] The scene is treated as a sad but necessary act, yet tragically it largely ignores the likely fatal consequences for an undomesticated animal raised by humans and abandoned with neither the skills nor experience to survive on its own in the wild.

In his 1966 *Rascal* follow-up, *Raccoons Are the Brightest People*, North chronicled dozens of other people's stories about pet raccoons, but again, with little assessment of the long-term consequences of turning wild animals into pets. And his books were followed by a slow but steady stream of stories of varying quality telling about mischievous raccoons who teach their human companions about life and loss. In spite of increasing legislation banning raccoons as pets, these tales continue to appear today, especially with ready access to online vanity publishing and distribution platforms. It is a depressing genre as a whole, as most of the animals end up as little more than footnotes in earnest but uncritical human improvement narratives, with the stories' endings almost invariably tragic for the raccoons themselves.

In some tales, the danger is to the humans rather than the raccoons. A. Lee Martinez's 2010 satirical fantasy *Divine Misfortune* features a world similar to our own, but with the addition of gods of past and present that are very much alive in mundane twenty-first-century modernity, inflicting misery and blessings in equal measure on the unfortunate mortals they encounter, most of whom just try to get along without drawing too much divine attention their way. Martinez's tongue-in-cheek tale follows a handful of human characters in their interactions with a diverse array of problematic deities, including a lower-level trickster raccoon god of fortune with the formal name of Luca (but who prefers the more approachable moniker of Lucky). When ordinary suburbanites Teri and Phil decide they need a little luck in their lives they take the raccoon god as their patron, unaware of the vengeful divine enemies he has made over the years, especially Gorgoz, a murderous and ancient being who suddenly takes an unhealthy interest in the couple. As befits a light-hearted fantasy romp where carnage is leavened throughout by laughter, Lucky's raccoonish cleverness serves him and his hapless followers rather well by the end, but ultimately Teri and Phil find that having a raccoon in the house, divine or otherwise, is far more of a headache than a help.

Sometimes raccoons take on a decidedly darker tone in the literature, especially in poetry. Stanley Kunitz's poem 'Raccoon

Journal' chronicles the relentless advance of a group of raccoons who have laid claim to the human habitations of Provincetown, on Cape Cod, Massachusetts. At first the poem seems to be a homeowner's response to increasingly irritating wildlife encounters. Yet as it proceeds the speaker's tone shifts from admiring to frustrated, even fearful. These raccoons are rendered as a gang of nocturnal rowdies who menace both the human and other-than-human animals of Provincetown in equal measure.

Gradually the speaker sees a kind of primal kinship with the raccoons, but not one he welcomes. There is no safe place in this human town; there is nowhere that the raccoons cannot claim as their own. Civilization is a facade; the world belongs to the raccoons. The teasing mockery of previous stanzas becomes a scene of primal horror at the end as they gather on his porch, 'half churring, half growling, / bubbling to a manic hoot / that curdles the night air'. One animal is splayed hanging on his door screen, looking in, while others gather in the darkness behind, and the final lines are a fatalistic revelation: 'They watch me, unafraid. / I know they'll never leave; / They've come to take possession.'[17]

Raccoons even appear as erotic interests. Beatriz Hausner's *Enter the Raccoon*, a book-length surrealist meditation on the passionate love affair between an unnamed woman and a human-sized raccoon, has the quality of a fever dream, but one that never strays too far from the biological reality of raccoons, to often-uncomfortable effect. Similarly, in a banned Russian anthology of erotic fiction, a South American crab-eating raccoon features as part of an interspecies threesome; it was one of the two stories the publisher's lawyers deemed pornographic, and the book's distribution was cancelled.[18]

Yet some writers find kinship of a different kind in this particular animal subject. In an exceptionally compassionate poem, Gerry LaFemina's 'The Raccoon', a hungry female raccoon's

The association between wilderness and raccoons looms large in this 1918 cover of *Boys' Life Magazine* from the Boy Scouts of America.

scavengings are empathetically compared to those of the speaker. While their neighbours fear that the raccoon's daylight appearances indicate rabies or other illness, the speaker and companions 'believed / different, understood what a cruel god hunger / can be, demanding we find food no matter what the risk'. The speaker tells of his own struggles with hunger, of dining-and-dashing, of the dismissive scorn and disregard of well-fed neighbours. He ends with a sympathetic admission about his bond with this vulnerable but determined creature:

And yes – I fed her; everyday
I hefted a bowl of sweet cereal, left it beside the door

and watched through a window
as she ate the red, green, and yellow rings.
I carried that bowl out

despite complaining neighbors – despite, even,
the continuation of raids against my trash.
I carried that bowl in my supplicant's fingers

like a present or an offering
for benevolence. I carried it forward
as if it were sacred.[19]

The bowl of cereal becomes not only a gift of food but an affirmation of kinship, and the speaker recognizes the duality of shared struggle and stigma. This raccoon's status is seemingly a far cry from that held by her procyonid ancestors among the Mississippian peoples, but the memory endures in this intimate recognition ceremony. The anomaly here, then, is not so much the raccoon herself as her species' place in the human imagination. The speaker's refusal to deny that bond brings a level of empathy to this raccoon–human relationship that is sadly rare in the literature – and, increasingly, in everyday life.

3 The Racist Coon

oh coon
which gave my grandfather a name
and fed his wife on more than one
occasion
i can no more change my references
than they can theirs
Lucille Clifton, 'what spells raccoon to me'[1]

In 2015 a controversy erupted in the U.S. when Dr Anthea Butler, an African American professor in the Department of Religious Studies at the University of Pennsylvania, was attacked by right-wing media for suggesting on Twitter that Black Republican and then-presidential candidate Ben Carson be given a 'Coon of the Year' award for stating in an interview that audience display of the white supremacist Confederate flag at National Association for Stock Car Auto Racing (NASCAR)-sponsored events was an exercise of private property rights. Most coverage failed to address the vagueness of the actual tweet, the specific political, historical or cultural context of the term within African American discourse, the ugly association of the Confederate flag with anti-Black racism in the U.S., or Carson's long advocacy of policies deemed by many as harmful to other African Americans. Instead, the largely white commentators of right-leaning media accused Butler of hypocrisy as a progressive Black woman with a distinguished history of anti-racist scholarship and activism for using this highly charged term in reference to a Black man whose conservative politics she opposed.

It is hardly so simple. 'Coon' elicits very different responses depending on its use and its audience. When referring to raccoons themselves – or to the Maine Coon cats, coonhounds and coon hunts named after them – the clipped *'coon* evokes the animals in

The anti-Black 'coon' stereotype is an insistently dehumanizing set of images and associations, ranging from bestial conflation with raccoons themselves to invocations of the history of enslaved labour, or both, as in this early twentieth-century coloured art card.

the context of rural life and culture, the challenge of hunting a furtive animal in the darkness of swamp and forest, with young Americans coming of age and coming to an understanding of life and death through the destined fate of their pursued quarry . . . the location, in mainstream depictions, being almost entirely one of unremarked-upon whiteness. When referring to humans, its most provoking use is as a widely taboo epithet used by white people to abuse African Americans in the racist vocabulary of the United States (and increasingly applied against other racialized minorities throughout the world).

Yet among African Americans it has other important meanings and nuances, as in the controversy cited above, where 'coon' has, like other terms of bigotry and abuse, been repurposed within specific African American cultural and political meanings. Butler's use of the term was firmly within this latter context, as *Slate* writer Chauncey DeVega notes, where coons are those 'who have been perceived as betraying the humanity, progress, self-respect, and dignity of Black America', invariably to curry white favour and upholding racist power structures.[2] As such, even if taken at face value, Butler's tweet would be far from hypocrisy – she would instead be calling out Carson's own mercenary respectability politics in sacrificing other Black people for personal advancement, and she used a term that had significance within her own community. This nuanced and culturally specific context for the term was either lost or ignored by reactionary commentators, and in the fallout Butler endured weeks of violent, racist harassment and threats.

The cultural history of raccoons is, perhaps surprisingly, inextricably connected to human race relations, predominantly in the United States but elsewhere in the world, and we will see those intersecting influences, currents and contexts emerge repeatedly in this volume. This is nowhere more evident than with 'coon', a term every bit as complex and provocative as its animal counterpart. Yet there are surprisingly few substantive considerations of the term and its social and political significance in the raccoon literature. A survey of scientific, historical and mainstream raccoon studies – largely by white writers and scholars – gestures to considerable discomfort in discussing this context in anything other than broad strokes and vague acknowledgements. This unfortunately means that the important lessons from that history are avoided, too. In this chapter we will focus entirely on this term's complex history and ongoing legacies, which will inform our subsequent discussions of raccoon representation.

Note: images in the current chapter will focus on broader political contexts, as the violently degrading images that so often accompany the coon stereotype do not require reproduction here. The most troubling relevant images from this ugly archive will be described, not illustrated, and only to the degree necessary for reader understanding.

In spite of attempts to trace its origins, the etymological divergence of 'coon' from 'raccoon' remains opaque, in part because it is an accretive term and set of associations layered over time and in response to diverse references, cultural contexts, language patterns, historical events, and changing politics and economics. We start, then, with the word 'raccoon' itself – or, rather, the short form of it. Word clipping is a common linguistic practice, and 'raccoon' itself is already a clipped, Anglicized form of the aforementioned Powhatan *arakun*; 'coon', then, is yet another natural short form, a fore-clipping with the softer initial sounds dropped and the more pronounced final syllable retained.

It was not just the English who readily adopted the clipped form of 'coon'; African American culinary historian and writer

Michael W. Twitty has suggested that it would have been a natural linguistic choice for enslaved West Africans brought to North America in whose varied languages the 'r' of raccoon is uncommon.[3] The first enslaved Africans to come to Jamestown colony in Powhatan territory were indeed from present-day Angola on the southwest part of the continent, and their 1619 arrival was within just a few years of 'raccoon' entering the English colonial vernacular. It is not unreasonable to conjecture that, through existing Indigenous trade routes and linguistic exchanges, along with the influence of English and the ever-expanding enslavement economy, the clipped 'coon' in reference to the animals themselves would have spread widely throughout the multiracial colonies, to the point that, by 1742, it makes an appearance in a diary entry from Joshua Hempstead, a white Connecticut landowner, indicating widespread use across racial, cultural and regional lines.[4]

'Coon' as a term for human beings dates at least to the late eighteenth century, when it was largely associated with shrewd rural whites. In the mid-1700s U.S., drawing on the popular presumptions about raccoon cleverness and their association with the wilderness, the contraction 'coon' in reference to a human being was a 'term for a white rustic', which evolved by the 1820s to 'a cunning or remarkable man'.[5] The 'rustic' association is unsurprising; by the American War of Independence (1775–83) white colonists had fully embraced the abundant indigenous raccoon as a malleable symbol of the masculinist American frontier, untouched by the corrupting urbanity and class hierarchies of the decadent European powers.

Human coons in the literature and folklife of the late eighteenth century and early nineteenth century were therefore widely understood as extensions of those associations: shrewd and independent backwoods or frontier whites, typically men, whose slightly antisocial cleverness made them more objects of admiration and

While 'coon' is still a regional form of reference to the animals themselves, as in this 1940s produce label from Louisiana, it has also long been a vexed and deeply racialized term in much of the U.S. and Canada.

good-natured fun than of scorn, especially when the elite were the target of their quick wit and questionable integrity. These were ambitious independent agents without inherited privileges or wealth; more negatively, they could be hucksters and confidence men whose natural guile brought them successfully through scrapes with the more sophisticated establishment. The self-made Tennessee frontiersman, raconteur and politician David 'Davy' Crockett was admiringly if somewhat condescendingly referred to by his white contemporaries as 'a right smart coon' in 1832, an association that he put to political effect in his re-election campaign to the U.S. House of Representatives in 1833. (It was likely only in political campaigning as a backwoods everyman that he wore the coonskin cap for which he would ever after be known.)

As the U.S. political and economic situation stabilized and power increasingly centred in and around eastern cities, the frontier symbols of that earlier period resonated less with the changing times, or at least became more markedly ambivalent. The raccoon was among the most diminished symbols. The humble and perhaps too familiar raccoon of previous generations could hardly compete with the stories of grander and more exotic animals like grizzly bears and bison now encountered on the ever-expanding western frontier of the Louisiana Purchase. Nor was it equal in standing to those elevated wildlife icons like the bald eagle that hearken back to great empires like Rome and Greece. The raccoon shifted from the colonial-era symbol of natural rights and roguish resistance to a representative of rustic simplicity or even coarse, untrustworthy degeneracy – hardly a respectable symbol for an ambitious young country determined to show itself an equal in the global family of imperial nations. And it is no surprise that this diminishment among white elites was accompanied by their increasing association of raccoons with Blackness.

The raccoon declined as a national symbol, and so did its white human counterpart, but the word 'coon' remained, although its meaning, like that of its animal referent, shifted as well. Related to the Spanish *barraca* and English 'barracks' for slave quarters or even a cage for transporting enslaved people, the Portuguese word *barracoon* is occasionally cited as the source for the racist use of 'coon', but this contemporaneous term seems to be a coincidental association that built on existing etymological foundations. Rather, the epithet can be more dependably traced to two intersecting cultural currents of the early nineteenth century: blackface minstrelsy and the Whig vs Democrat American party politics of the decades leading to the U.S. Civil War.

Raccoon, a comic character and 'old debauchee' in the first U.S. opera, *The Disappointment; or, The Force of Credulity* (1767), is the proud but foolish target of the confidence scam that serves as the performance's thin plot. He has occasionally been cited as the first representation of a Black character in American theatre (notably, a free Black man), but other scholars have convincingly argued that contemporary audiences would more likely have read him as either French or Pennsylvania Dutch, not Black, as his accent and mannerisms are more in keeping with stereotypes of eccentric European foreigners than of African Americans in that era.[6]

The first clearly documented association between the roguish coon figure and African Americans was the 1834 minstrel song 'Zip Coon', by the white singer-songwriter George Washington Dixon, who may have appropriated and popularized a song already in circulation. Featuring white performers in burnt-cork blackface caricaturing African American culture, music and dance, minstrel shows became increasingly popular after the Civil War but had a significant presence before that conflict. White performers took on an exaggerated dialect and costumes that mocked Black peoples' intellect and moral character, and portrayed them as ignorant, lazy and lecherous, but largely unthreatening. (After the Emancipation Proclamation of 1863, the stereotypes on stage become increasingly menacing, with paranoid insistence on enacted or latent threats of Black violence against whites, and especially the spectre of Black men threatening white womanhood.) In the early nineteenth century, these stereotypes were a bit more unstable than they would be even a few decades later, and Zip Coon offers troubling insight into that history.

There were two dominant white stereotypes of Black men on stage and in print during the nineteenth century: Zip Coon and Jim Crow. They emerged together in the 1830s as parallel white representations of Black degradation, becoming more exaggerated over time. While Jim Crow was a condescending stereotype of plantation primitivism as a lazy and unkempt simpleton slave,

the urban, arrogant Zip Coon offered another aggressively negative image. American studies scholar Psyche Williams-Forson
observes that 'Zip Coon made a mockery out of blacks who had
any kind of aspirations – economic, political, social, or cultural.'[7]
As a northern Black dandy – cultivated, well-dressed and insistent
on his rightful place among the cultured and elite – Zip Coon was
a primary target for racist fury, for his refusal to accept an inferior
social or economic status made him particularly dangerous to
ever-anxious white supremacy. White minstrels countered his
social threat by portraying his dignity as pretence, and on the
stage and page he became a foppish freedman fool presenting
himself as the equal of whites when, under white supremacy, his
social position was meant to be one of servile debasement. In a
later word also deeply imbricated in racist ideology, Zip Coon is
the epitome of 'uppity', a Black inferior daring to presume social
equality with whites and inevitably falling short.

To many whites of the time, African Americans were quite
simply figured as a lower order of humanity – or not entirely
human at all, as indicated by their animalistic association with
the degraded Crow and absurd Coon. Another animal reference
specific to Zip Coon is the eponymous character's jacket – the
'long-tail'd blue', which would have been recognizable to theatre-
goers of the time as a reference to the blue jay, a brightly plumaged,
garrulous corvid relative of the crow often characterized as a
beautiful but obnoxiously loud bird. Cultural historian Barbara
Lewis adds:

Jim Crow, whose popularity whirled through the nation
beginning in 1829, provided a welcome answer to what
was to be done with Blue's audacity and arrogance. Crow,
as one bird to another, dragged down Long Tail Blue's
perky feathers. Crow was not in the same class as Blue, who

gloried in his plumage; Crow was a much commoner sort of bird, but he was the one to get the job done. By parodying Blue, being crooked instead of straight and rag-tag instead of debonair, Crow threw a crimp into Blue's style, arresting his upward movement . . . Zip Coon, who also premiered in song and whose misshapen image decorated a cover sheet, finished the job of clipping Blue's wings, ensuring that he would never again rise out of the ranks of meniality. If Crow served as the antithesis to Blue, Coon mixed their individual elements into a scoundrel composite, the gangling servant dressed in the master's clothes. Coon combined the original and its reverse into a mockery of the former.[8]

Representations of Black animality are already well in development by the 1830s, becoming more extreme and concretized in subsequent decades.

The original 1834 sheet music cover of 'Zip Coon' shows a prim Black dandy in fashionable attire, one hand on his hip, swinging a pair of glasses on a chain and looking directly at the viewer with haughty regard. The bedraggled Crow and presumptuous Coon were not simply circulating as period contemporaries – they served as mutually reinforcing images in the racist white imaginary. Roland Leander Williams reads Zip Coon in these productions as 'a scoundrel who made freedom look like a bad thing for black men . . . an image of a profane and defiant black wretch'.[9] The figure's name, too, carries derisive meaning: 'Zip' is a corruption of 'Scipio' (for the Roman general Scipio Africanus), one of many Classical names imposed by white slaveholders on enslaved African Americans as a mocking invocation of Greek and Roman slaveholding and its presumed centrality to early democracy. The twisted implication here is that slavery bestows purpose and

By the mid-19th century, whites used the racist minstrel figure of Zip Coon to mock African American social and economic advancement. As legalized segregation became entrenched across the U.S., Zip Coon became an increasingly exaggerated and grotesque caricature.

elevation – thus *Scipio* – that becomes degraded to the uncouth *Zip* in that institution's absence.

Other performers released alternative versions of Dixon's popularized minstrel tune. Some skewered the political pretensions of 'backwoods' white men like the aforementioned Davy Crockett as well as upwardly mobile free northern Blacks, as in Thomas Birch's 1834 contribution to the emergent Zip Coon song genre:

An de bery nex President, will be Zip Coon.

An wen Zip Coon our President shall be,
He make all de little Coons sing posum up a tree;
O how de little Coons, will dance an sing,
Wen he tie dare tails togedder, cross de lim dey swing.

Now mind wat you arter, you tarnel kritter Crocket,
You shant go head widout old Zip, he is de boy to block it,
Zip shall be President, Crocket shall be vice,
An den dey two togedder, will hab de tings nice.[10]

Both Zip Coon and the coonskin-capped Crocket are dismissed
as similarly absurd figures. And although the representation of
Zip Coon is explicitly insulting, the actual term 'coon' had not yet
fully ossified into a wholly racist epithet; in 1834 it is as much a
classist insult about these two ostensibly unsophisticated coons
– one obscure and Black, one famous and white – who are wholly
unfit for the dignity of the high office and high society to which
they aspire.

As a symbol the raccoon would, for a short time at least,
resemble that of the clever fox or trickster coyote – slightly unsavoury, not entirely trustworthy, but amusing and even
admirable in its own way. Zip Coon is ridiculously pretentious
but also audacious, and while his boastful ambition for the u.s.
presidency with the famous Crockett as his white subordinate is
treated as comic, it is also, within the politics of the time, surprisingly bold – and dangerous to the social order. 'Coon' is already
taking on racist associations and meanings, but still maintains
class critique that could yet be applied to whites; within little
more than a decade this would change as it became an exclusively
racist term.

This was heralded by the 1828 election of Andrew Jackson to the presidency, which signalled a major change in U.S. politics, as he was the first president who came from outside the privileged circle of the celebrated 'Founding Fathers', and Jacksonian politics are central to the rise of coon as a national racist epithet. Like his political opponent Davy Crockett, and like the raccoons taken up as a state symbol by its settler citizenry, Jackson was associated with the white frontiersmen of rural Tennessee, and his politics were explicitly rooted in white populism. Jackson's own story of impoverished childhood to controversial military service to national political leadership made him well regarded among voters outside New England, who chafed against what they saw as the oversized influence and inherited privileges and wealth of the northern Founders and their home states. It was in the Jacksonian era that party politics emerged in the U.S. – anathema to George Washington and his partisan peers, who foresaw the danger of political loyalty going to party and personality over nation. Jackson's supporters founded the Democratic Party in the lead-up to the 1828 election, while his opponents coalesced into the Whig Party in the 1830s, seeing in Jackson's expansionist ideology and populism an existential threat to the constitutional republic. The conflict between the two parties continued well after Jackson left the White House in 1837.

The complex politics of the time are beyond the scope of this discussion, but 1840 is when we return to raccoons, for it is in this year that Jackson's politically weak Democratic successor, Martin Van Buren, was defeated in the presidential election by the Whig candidate William Henry Harrison. While Van Buren had genuinely risen from poverty to political prominence like his predecessor Jackson, it was the wealthy and well-connected scion Harrison who excited the public imagination as the every-man candidate, even going so far as to appropriate the derisive statement by a Democratic editor that suggested he retire to a log cabin and drink his remaining days away in obscurity.

Harrison and his supporters used the 'log cabin and hard cider' campaign slogan and mobilized other common-man iconography to highlight his constructed plebian credentials in opposition to Van Buren's supposed elitism. And as coonskin caps were still associated with the virtues of frontier simplicity in some vote-rich rural areas, they became a feature of Harrison's campaign rallies:

The Harrison log cabin, hard cider and raccoon are featured on this c. 1840–45 appliqué cotton quilt panel, likely by Rebecca Diggs of Maryland.

the eagerness of the Whig party to identify with rural white common people led it to adopt symbols like Davy Crockett's coonskin cap and . . . to nail coonskins to supporters' cabin doors and to use live coons as signs of party loyalty. Thus Whigs also became 'coons', especially in the speech of Democrats, who cursed Whigs in 'coongress'

and Whig 'coonventions', Whig 'coonism' and a lack of Whig 'coonsistency'.[11]

Harrison died within a month of taking office, and his successor, John Tyler, so alienated other Whigs during his single term that in 1844 Henry Clay was nominated instead as the Whig candidate for president.

Clay happily continued the 'log cabin campaign' approach of Harrison, and once again took a Democratic insult as his slogan: with a string of unsuccessful runs for president or party nominee, shifting positions on numerous policy issues, and political compromises that seemed more about self-interest than principle, Clay was derisively dismissed as the 'same old coon' by his opponents. Like Harrison, Clay embraced the association, and Whig campaign banners, flyers, leather balls, ribbons and other campaign paraphernalia soon featured abundant raccoons extolling the virtues of the 'Old Kentucky Coon' and his party, put to service in Clay's self-fashioning of himself as a modest, determined and consistent champion of the common people against what was now viewed as Democratic tyranny.

As the wealthy Clay embraced the raccoon as his own everyman symbol, his opponents found it useful as well; two Democratic papers from Ohio – the *Coon Dissector* and *Ohio Coon Catcher* – were among the many virulently anti-Whig publications of the time, and featured illustrations of raccoons being subjected to various forms of violence, including being treed, hanged, starved and skinned. Clay narrowly lost to the Democratic candidate, James Polk; his Whig Party continued to be a political force, but its influence dwindled, ending in the 1850s with the emergence of the Republican Party. And just as the political parties were changing, the 'same old coon' was changing, too, and in deeply troubling ways.

The three key Whig symbols from William Henry Harrison's successful 1840 presidential campaign were recycled for Henry Clay's own failed 1844 run, as seen in this page from the *National Clay Minstrel, and Frelinghuysen Melodist* (1843), a collection of Whig campaign songs.

101

THE 'COON SONG.
Written for the National Clay Minstrel.
TUNE,—" *Dandy Jim of Caroline.*"

A race, a race! And who will win?
Who will be out? who will be in?
Trot out your nags! we'll see who'll take
From all, the Presidential stake.
   The people say, they'll go for Clay,
   The true heart's hope, the country's stay;
   So raise the shout, and clear the way,
   For work and worth and Harry Clay!

During the 1844 presidential campaign the avowedly Democratic newspaper the *Coon Dissector* featured Whiggish raccoons suffering a range of torments, often at the beak and claw of wiry Democratic roosters.

Indeed, it is in that 1844 presidential campaign that the racist coon is firmly established. Clay, himself a slaveholder who nevertheless declared his philosophical opposition to the institution, had been inconsistent on the question of Texas annexation and its status as a future slave state. Democrats, then a fiercely pro-slavery party, blasted him in the press as a hypocrite and a closet

COON DISSECTOR.

Vol. I. Dayton, Friday, June 28, 1844. No. 6.

THE COON DISSECTOR

IS PUBLISHED
EVERY FRIDAY MORNING
BY A. H. MUNN:
At the Western Empire Office corner of Main and New Market streets.

TERMS.

Thirty copies for	$15,00
Twenty " "	12,00
Fifteen, " "	8,00
Ten, " "	6,00

THE BARGIN AND SALE. PROOF AS STRONG AS HOLY WRIT.

Clay is guilty of a corrupt coalition with Adams by his silent confession. Gen. Jackson and Mr. McDuffie declare they can substantiate the charge to the credence of any jury. When Clay was in the Capitol at Washington City lately, Col. Bony of Kentucky, on the floor of Congress declared that Clay wrote a letter to Mr. Blair of the Globe to get Adams elected, & that he (Clay) would be made Sec. of State, when it was well known that the Kentucky members were instructed for Gen. Jackson. Blair has the letter, and Clay *dare* not call for its publication. Col. Boyd called for Ex-Speaker White, Clay's *friend*, to write for liberty to have that letter published. *White sneaked off.* Now for facts:

Adams and Clay were bitter enemies in 1822, '3 '4. Clay give Adams the *lie* as to matters concerning the treaty of Ghent. The question of veracity has never been settled so far as the public knows. Col. Boyd says:

Hence when Clay and his friends in congress voted for Adams, the excitement among the people as can easily be imagined was prodigious. Even after four years had passed away and notwithstanding the gigantic efforts of Clay and his friends to sustain Adams, so firmly *did* the people of Kentucky believe that that gentleman was truly, both in practice and in theory, a genuine federalist, and an enemy of the West, [and I think their opinion to this day remains unchanged in both respects,] that in 1828, he was beaten by General Jackson for the Presidency, by the large majority of 7,901 votes. * *

In 1828, the general excitement on the account of the vote of Mr. Clay and his friends for Mr. Adams was great, and the charge of corrupt bargain between Mr. Adams and Mr. Clay was so pointed and openly made, that the senate of Kentucky was induced to take up and investigate the subject: persons and papers were sent for, &c.; and of the testimony given before that body, the following is a part.

Hon. John T. Johnson, brother of Col. R. M. Johnson, and at that time a member of Congress, stated that "he was then at Washington city in 1824, and at the time of the Presidential election in Feb. 1825. After the election he and his brother [Col. J.] were in company with Gen. Metcalfe, who told them he had a letter from Kentucky, which stated that the people would be dissatisfied with the result. His brother told the general that this voting for Mr. Adams would be an uphil business in Kentucky. The general replied, '*I fear we have done too much for our friend.*'" He was asked whether he did hear Mr. White, one of the members of Congress who voted for Adams, say, a few days after the election, that he was considered, when voting for Mr. Adams, that he was voting for Mr. Clay. This question was objected to, and overruled; 14 to 19.

Mr. McMillian, of the House of Representatives, stated, in reply to interrogatories, that Mr. Francis Johnson was at "Tompkinsville, in Monroe county, after his return home, subsequently to the presidential election, where he was asked how he came to vote for Mr. Adams. Mr. Johnson answered that he voted for Mr. Adams to get Mr. Clay made Secretary of State. He made this declaration repeatedly in conversation, and witnessed belief of in a public speech. He said Mr. Adams for President and Mr. Clay for his Secretary, would conduce more to the interests of the West, than Gen. Jackson President, with we know not whom for his Secretary; and that Clay might perhaps succeed him."

David Trimble, member of Congress, said, and declared to John Mason witness:

"He knew Adams to be an *apostate federalist*, and that if he ever voted for him, witness might call him a federalist as long as he lived. He also said, that Adams had agreed to give up the navigation of the Mississippi for whales and mackerel, and that [Adams] had always been an *enemy to the West*." When witness heard that Trimble had voted for Adams he was surprised; and soon after his return he had a conversation with him about his vote, in which he gave as his reasons that "We ascertained if Adams was made president Clay would be made Sec. of State; that if Gen. Jackson was made President, Clay would not be made Secretary; and that it would be better for us to have Adams, with Clay Secretary, than Gen. Jackson without him."

Of the mass of testimony other than that taken before the Senate, the following affidavit is a specimen:

"We the subscribers certify on oath, that we were severally present at the Lewis county court, for October, 1825, and heard David Trimble make a speech, and he used the following language. "When we went on last fall to the city of Washington, we found Crawford out of the question; the question was between Gen. Jackson and John Quincy Adams. We ascertained that under no circumstances, would Gen. Jackson appoint our friend Clay, Secretary of State. Knowing this, then, fellow citizens, that Gen. Jackson would not, and Mr. Adams would appoint our friend Henry Clay Secretary of State, and if you expected me to vote for Gen Jackson you expected me to do that which I could not and would not do.

Signed,
JACOB FRIZZLE,
DENRY HALBERT,
DAVID C. HEATH,
WM. C. COFFRIN,
RICHARD PELL,
JOHN HENDRICK,
JESSE HAMRICK,
JOHN GRIFFITH,
WM. DAVIS,
HEZ GRIFFITH,
WM. HAMBLIN,
DAVID TONKRY."

Clay in 1817 made a speech in favor of *instructions*, but he violated them when he was instructed, to go for Gen. Jackson. So decisively in favor of Gen. Jackson was the *will* of the people of Kentucky in 1824 '25 that only eleven members of the House of Representatives out of 84, present, voted against the declaratory resolution, to that effect—and of that eleven not one based his vote on the allegation that the resolution was not true.

You ask what were the facts in reference to the instructions of the legislature of Kentucky in 1841 '42 on the subject of the bankrupt law. The leading facts are as follows: On the 9th January, 1842, the Kentucky House of Representatives adopted the following resolutions unanimously, or, at least, without a division, viz:

"1st. *Resolved*, That in the opinion of the general assembly of the commonwealth of Kentucky, it is the desire of a large majority of the people of Kentucky, that the bankrupt law, enacted at the late extra session of Congress shall be repealed.

"2d. *Resolved, further*, That our senators in Congress be and they are hereby instructed, and our Representatives requested to use their influence to have the said law repealed."

Notwithstanding the decisive action of the legislature, the unanimity of the Kentucky members of the other House and the declarations of his colleague and friend in the Senate, all evincing, beyond a doubt that the will of his constituents, Mr. Clay voted against the repeal.

It is but just to Mr. Clay to state the reasons which induced him to disregard the will of his constituents, so unequivocally made known to him. They were, that the bankrupt law was a part of the whig system, which he wished to preserve entire; and that he could not, and would not, be instrumental in taking from the bankrupt the relief which he had been promised.

These grounds for disobedience are found distinctly stated in a speech delivered by him in the Senate on the 28th of January, 1842. Having adverted to the extra session of 1841, and its measures—the incorporation of a national bank, the distribution law, the increase of the tariff, the bankrupt law, and the relief of the banks in the District of Columbia—he said:—

"These were the fruits of the extra session, so far as they depended upon Congress. This was the circle of beneficent measures, intended to embrace all interests and all parts of the Union. It was a GREAT SYSTEM, parts of which were more or less adapted to all portions of the Union. We have reason to believe that it was looked upon and regarded as a *whole*; and that votes were given for some measures in the series, not so much because they were in consonance with the views of the constituents whose members gave these votes, as because they were wanted by other parts of the Union, and the compensation was found in other more respectable measures of the same series."

This practice of *buying votes for measures* not "in consonance with the views of the constituency," however well adapted to the promotion of purposes of ambition, is totally subversive of the right of instruction, if not of all purity in legislation.—And at the close of the speech delivered by Clay in opposition to the repeal of the bankrupt law, he said; "And I am invited to unite in this work of inhumanity and cruelty; I have not the heart to do it! I have not the head to do it! I cannot, *I will not do it!*"

Stripped of its poetry this declaration means, "I am called upon by my constituents to vote for a repeal of the bankrupt law: *I will not do it!*"

After a few remarks from Mr. Benton for, and Mr. Williams against the repeal, the vote on the bill from the House of Representatives repealing the bankrupt law was taken, and resulted as follows—yeas 22, nays 23:

Those who voted in the affirmative, were Messrs. Allen, Archer, Bayard, Benton, Buchanan, Calhoun, Fulton, Graham, King, Linn, McRoberts, Morehead, Pierce, Prentiss, Rives, Sevier, Smith of Connecticut, Sturgeon, Woodbury, Wright, and Young.

Those who voted in the negative, were Messrs. Barrow, Bates, Berrien, Choate, CLAY, Clayton, Evans, Henderson, Huntington, Kerr, Mangum, Merrick, Miller, Phelps, Porter, Simmons, Smith of Indiana, Southard, Tallmadge, Walker, White, Williams, and Woodbridge.

You will see that the fate of the bill depended on Mr. Clay's vote; and had he obeyed the will of his constituents, that wholesale repudiation of honest debts, which disgraced the year 1842, would never have occurred, as the bankrupt law had not then gone into operation.

Very respectfully,
Your obedient servant,
LINN BOYD.

Messrs. W. Coles and G. W. Hopkins.

WHIG PROMISES FOR 1844.

The Whig papers are beginning to repeat the humbugging promises of prosperity in the event of Clay's election, which they made in 1840. The Wabash Courier of May 11th says—

"With Henry Clay President, the country will prosper—Industry will be rewarded—Enterprise directed moderately, to proper channels, will be encouraged and receive its just dues. All branches of business, acting and reacting, though each first for itself, yet all for the whole—mutually and reciprocally aiding each other most flourish. The prosperity of one, as almost necessary consequence, under the influence of a proper Tariff, and a steady National Currency, will be the aid and support of another, through the great series of ramified business over our wide extended country."

This is the kind of gammon by which thousands were deluded in 1840, but it will hardly go down this year. They are too much like Bank promises to pay—made to gull, and be broken.—[State Sentinel.

The New York Plebeian says the whigs are destined to be devoured bodily by the democrats in less than six months. Well, if such is our destiny, we must submit to it. It is the fate of all mortals to be eaten by vermin sooner or later.—*Prentice's Jour.*

Yes, but it is by no means the fate of all mortals to eat such vermin as the *coons*.—We protest against dining with the Plebian. If the Louisville editor expects the honor of being eaten by democrats, that is not the entertainment to which we wish invited. Faugh!—[Boston Post.

Fixed at last!—On last Saturday, our fellow citizen Mr. Gideon B. Polk, "accidentally found within a tombstone, in the grave-yard in this place the money which was taken from the Branch of the Union Bank at Columbia—in 1834. Some six thousand dollars of the money was in a good state of preservation and is as good as ever. The rest however, was so rotten as to be entirely useless—and in fact, was so rotten that the amount could not be ascertained. Various conjectures exist as to how it came there, but nothing is known with the least certainty. Mr. Polk gave up the money to the Bank as he found it.—[Tennessee Democrat.

It is thought that the reason why Mr. Clay left Washington so suddenly and sloped home so silently, was his having picked up a democratic newspaper in which he discovered Jackson's opinion of him:

"Under such circumstances *how contemptible* does this *demagogue* appear, when he descends from his high place and roams about the country retailing slanders upon the living and the dead."

General Clay!—The Portsmouth Tribune has an engraving under its editorial head representing Henry Clay, in the Revolutionary War, with sword in one hand and banner in the other, taking a British vessel in the distance. We give it up now! Gen. Clay, of the American Revolution!—That *is* the finish!

☞ The K. in Col. Polk's name is understood to stand for "Koonkiller."

SPIRIT OF 1840.

Long after his 1844 defeat, Whig Party presidential candidate Henry Clay continued to be caricatured as the 'Same Old Coon'. From Henry Louis Stephens's *The Comic History of the Human Race*; colour lithograph by L. Rosenthal, 1851.

abolitionist, which cost him support from long-distrustful southern Whigs. With the Old Kentucky Coon represented as an abolition sympathizer – and thus a sympathizer with African Americans – the coon became enmeshed with slavery, and by extension, with advocacy for African American rights and equality, which were anathema to white supremacists in both slave and free states.

As the issue of abolition grew more divisive in the lead-up to the U.S. Civil War, these various currents – the backward, ignorant and increasingly untrustworthy 'coon', Zip Coon and Jim Crow minstrelsy, white racial anxieties in reaction to Black advances, and so on – came together with increasing venom in North and South alike to reinforce white notions of Black inferiority. And raccoons once again feature in this narrative.

Even in the early nineteenth century, African Americans 'had long been popularly associated with the raccoon . . . the association was largely by way of the ascribed affection of blacks for the amiable and tasty little beasts. By ascription, blacks loved hunting, trapping, and eating raccoons.'[12] These associations were already common even among white Europeans who went hunting with their slaveholding white hosts:

> Unless animals such as raccoon and opossum posed a direct threat, [white] sportsmen generally felt that they offered inferior sport, so they pursued them only as a recreational novelty or as a piece of local color from the slave quarters. As indigenous species with no European counterparts, raccoon and opossum fell within the slave's

With brooms ready for sweeping away corruption, victorious Democratic roosters crow as a vice-ridden Henry Clay and his raccoonish Whig supporters lose the crucial state of New York in William Dohnert's cartoon commentary on the November 1844 presidential campaign.

The hard-fought 1860 U.S. presidential election inspired this political cartoon, which rallied liberal Whig sympathizers of a previous generation to Abraham Lincoln's upstart Republican Party against the establishment conservative Democrats.

Come gather, ye old boys of 1840,
Who rallied 'round Tippecanoe,
And raise up your hearts and your voices
For ABRAHAM, the honest and true.

domain. When white hunters blundered into a raccoon or opossum, they killed it, but they often turned the body over to their huntsmen because they considered these animals more suitable on a slave's table.[13]

Raccoons were also a source of accessible nutrition otherwise denied by slaveholders who used food access to reinforce domination; as hunting quarry they were thus in a real way linked to Black survival, and their relative abundance and availability to enslaved people threatened the resource-scarcity model imposed by slaveholders for control.

Although raccoon hunting was common among poor whites as well as Black Americans, in the literature of this period it is increasingly represented as a predominantly Black *recreational* activity, the raccoon dismissed as a comical and degraded hunting quarry, its important subsistence dimensions minimized, dismissed or ignored. Take, for instance, this passage from *The*

Steel-engraved scene of African American raccoon hunters on the banks of Virginia's Chickahominy River, by W. L. Sheppard and W. Wellstood, 1872.

Hunters' Feast; or, Conversations around the Camp-fire (1855), from the Irish American adventure writer Thomas Mayne Reid, which chronicles a plantation coon hunt and offers insight into these increasing conflations:

> There is a curious connection between the negro and the raccoon. It is not a tie of sympathy, but a link of antagonism. The 'coon, as already observed, is the negro's legitimate game. 'Coon-hunting is peculiarly a negro sport. The negro is the 'coon's mortal enemy. He kills the 'coon when and wherever he can, and eats it too. He loves its 'meat,' which is pork-tasted, and in young 'coons palatable enough, but in old ones rather rank. This, however, our 'darkie' friend does not much mind, particularly if his master be a 'stingy old boss,' and keeps him on rice instead of meat rations . . .
>
> The 'coon-hunt is a 'nocturnal' sport, and therefore does not interfere with the negro's regular labour. By right the night belongs to him, and he may then dispose of his time as he pleases, which he often does in this very way.[14]

The second paragraph merits particular attention here, as white commentators' identification of raccoons and enslaved African Americans with the night gradually takes on an insidious set of associations. Raccoons are no longer respectable or even admirable symbols of frontier pluck and verve. They have become pathetic scavengers who do their sneaky business at night and thrive on more respectable (white) people's labour; their terror when treed and surrounded by snarling enemies was an ignoble but suitable end for a now wholly vilified beast.

The nocturnal coon hunt is increasingly pathologized by white observers as a distracting recreational pursuit that diminishes slave work capacity. In other words, because they are perceived as being less productive daytime workers after a night of hunting, the narrative becomes about enslaved Black men stealing *their own labour* from white slaveowners, and doing so not for food but for trivial, even vulgar entertainment. By the 1850s, raccoons and African Americans are rendered in similarly degrading terms by white writers: the uncouth, sneaky raccoon who trespasses and raids farmers' fields and chicken coops at night rather than pursuing honest subsistence in the wild stands in parallel with the uncouth, untrustworthy slave who fritters away his nights hunting unsavoury quarry and avoiding his obligatory daytime field labour. The latter, too, as the human counterpart to the nocturnal robber raccoon, is frequently accused of stealing from white slaveholders, with a particular fixation on chickens and watermelons (both long-standing racist associations).[15]

The raccoon outlaw who raids chicken coops became a particularly ugly anti-Black symbol in the 19th-century U.S., and the racist associations continue to have currency with fringe white nationalist groups today.

In particular, the rooster as racist motif aligns closely with the way raccoons are figured in the white imaginary of the time. Just as Whigs embraced the raccoon as their symbol, southern white Democrats took up the rooster as their own, drawing on the above representational tradition to depict fierce and formidable cockerels fighting against menacing dark raccoons/coons; in newspapers like the aforementioned *Ohio Coon Catcher* the Democratic roosters were often featured in fierce pursuit of Whig raccoons or crowing proudly over their corpses. (Whigs were all too happy to acknowledge their opponents' choice of mascot, with partisans portraying scrawny Democratic roosters being throttled or otherwise menaced by grinning Whig raccoons.) In short order the Democratic rooster stood firmly for white supremacist, nativist and xenophobic politics, especially in the South; in 1904, when the Alabama Democratic Party decided on an official party symbol, they paired a crowing white rooster with the mottos 'White Supremacy' and 'For the Right', with racist supporters encouraged to 'Stamp Under the Rooster' on voting day.[16] While falling in prominence after the Civil Rights era of the 1960s, the white rooster has since been resurrected, most notoriously by the Proud Boys, a right-wing extremist group.

White roosters and hens were not the only poultry to be drafted into this racist iconography. To complicate matters further, African American men were represented as threatening, hypersexual black roosters and African American women as fecund egg-laying black hens in the late century, one more point where demeaning animalistic stereotypes overlap and reinforce one another. Whether four-footed or two-legged, the raccoon/coon is again figured explicitly as a socially, economically and even sexually dangerous outlaw, but only the human coon – being conceived also as property – is so degraded as to *steal and consume himself*. More specifically, as larcenous human coons, sexually

The White Women of Kentucky cannot afford to fail to vote. The Negro women are registering in large numbers and will vote SOLIDLY for the Republican ticket thus making

A Negro Vote of 150,000

and theirs will be the deciding vote in this election if the White Women Do Not Register and Vote The Straight Democratic Ticket

Under The

STAMP 🐓 ROOSTER

VOTE THIS WAY (X) UNDER THE ROOSTER

By the 1920s the rooster was a widely recognized symbol of white supremacy in the U.S. South. This poster was distributed to white women voters in Kentucky (most likely in 1922) to counter Black women's growing political power and influence.

dangerous cocks, and brooding hens who also eagerly kill and consume their (white) animal counterparts, there is the unmistakable savagist implication of cannibalism that firmly attaches to these anti-Black stereotypes, further deepening the white supremacist insistence on Black inhumanity. The accretion and interplay of all these bestial images thus enable 'coon' to be weaponized in multiple ways within the white supremacist social lexicon of the time.[17]

As former Whigs – among them, Abraham Lincoln – came to prominence in the new Republican Party, the layered associations of Whiggish 'coonism' returned, and it reached all the way to England. One well-publicized example occurred during the U.S. Civil War, in what would come to be known as the Trent Affair. In 1861 Union forces boarded the RMS *Trent*, a British ship, and took two Confederate diplomats prisoner. The act, while popular in the North, incensed the Confederacy and the British government alike. President Lincoln ultimately released the diplomats to avert conflict with the UK, but the move was unpopular among his own supporters, as it made him look weak at home and abroad. A January 1862 *Punch* cartoon by John Tenniel (famed illustrator of Lewis Carroll's *Alice* books) featured a treed raccoon with Lincoln's head, brow furrowed and face pensive, staring down at a rotund John Bull with rifle raised to blast his quarry from the branch.[18] The affair was widely seen as a national embarrassment, made all the more so by the mocking representation of Lincoln as a hunched raccoon quailing before a hunter's gun. The

Abraham Lincoln's handling of the Trent Affair brought him ridicule in Great Britain as well as the U.S., as demonstrated by Sir John Tenniel's unflattering 1862 *Punch* caricature of Lincoln as a pathetic raccoon treed by the hunter John Bull.

"Up a Tree"—From London Punch, January 11, 1862.

raccoon was no longer worthy of regard – it was now a quivering creature hardly fit for a noble hunter's bullet.

In the decades after the Civil War and Reconstruction, white supremacists in southern states imposed oppressive legal regimes of segregation, dispossession, disenfranchisement and state violence – later to be known as 'Jim Crow' laws – to halt Black economic, social and political advances. The choice of Jim Crow as the symbolic representation of legalized Black marginalization was not accidental, for the stereotype of the ignorant, lazy Black man was integral to justifying the continued subjugation of African Americans. By the end of the nineteenth century, as anti-Black stereotypes hardened among whites throughout the country, an entire musical form emerged that capitalized on and further entrenched these racist ideas: the ragtime 'coon song'.

Maurice B. Wheeler, a scholar of African American popular and historical music, observes that 'minstrelsy was the dominant popular American entertainment between the 1840s and the 1870s', yet the 'extreme financial hardships brought on by the [Civil War], and the economic depression that followed, resulted in a far more exaggerated negative tone to minstrel music'. In some regions African Americans competed with whites economically and with great success; as a result, the anti-Black stereotypes in minstrel music became increasingly hyperbolic and grotesque. Quite simply, 'the more white society saw itself losing control of blacks, the more minstrel music intensified in its criticism of them.'[19] The coon was one of many white categories of domination, and it again proved malleable for reinforcing those hierarchies.

Yet one of the unexpected features of the coon song craze was the role that African American performers played in its development. The first hit coon song, 'All Coons Look Alike to Me' (1895), was by the Black ragtime innovator Ernest Hogan, and many

ONE OF THE <u>YOUNG</u> BO-HOYS IN ECSTACIES BEFORE THE COONS OF 1844

In this lithograph, Whig raccoons plot an 1848 presidential comeback while playing a political tune for Horace Greeley, the powerful left-wing newspaper publisher who in 1846 helped defeat Silas Wright, the Democratic governor of New York.

other coon songs from the period were written and performed by Black musicians. There is much to be said about the genre and the complicated ways these songs responded to, challenged and simultaneously reified white racial attitudes about Black identities and experiences, especially when Black performers were part of the creation and presentation of the form, but as American studies scholar Patricia R. Schroeder reminds us, in these songs 'we see the challenges to dominant racist discourse, but we also see the traces of all that came before: of medicine shows, of the blues, of folk songs, toasts, and tall tales, of generations of playful parody and making a way from no way.'[20] In a time when Black performers had very few viable options for making a living on the stage, coon songs specifically written and performed by Black artists were one way to do so, presenting stereotypes to a paying white audience while subverting, even mocking, their expectations.

It was a delicate balance, however, and the popularity of the form made it inevitable that white songwriters and performers would stake claim to it, from all-male minstrelsy groups to women 'coon shouters' in blackface. The odious racism of many subsequent songs – accompanied with exaggeratedly bigoted imagery on the songbook covers – is far more extreme than Hogan's breakout hit or those of other Black songwriters. There were quite literally hundreds of these songs – Schroeder puts the number at more than six hundred – and some sold upwards of a million copies.[21] As a body of music they are gleefully racist, as indicated by the following representative sample: 'I'm Glad Dat Face Didn't Grow on Me', 'The Stuttering Coon: A Darktown Impediment', 'The Coffee Colored Coon: A Mocha-Java Importation', 'Mammy's Kinky-headed Coon', and, among the most appalling, 'I'm Gwine to Kill a Coon' (from the persona of a Black man threatening to 'carve' a dandified romantic rival with a knife), the murderous ballad of a jealous lover, 'She'll Never Live to Love Another Coon', and 'There'd Never Been No Trouble if They'd Kidnapped a Coon', in which the singer blithely affirms that the rightful uproar over a white child's disappearance would never have accompanied the kidnapping of a Black child.

Coon songs continued to be published and performed well into the 1930s, and their impact on racism and racial violence in the u.s. cannot be overestimated. Many were recorded but are largely inaccessible to all but scholars now. Even so, these songs did not operate in a representational vacuum. As white demand for coon songs grew, other popular culture arose that utilized both the term and raccoon/coon imagery, invariably reinforcing the link between African Americans and the exaggerated animalistic qualities discussed earlier, especially in lithographs, picture books and a wide range of ephemera.

A typical example is from white illustrator E. W. Kemble, best known today as the first illustrator of Mark Twain's *The Adventures of Huckleberry Finn* and, perhaps surprisingly, Harriet Beecher Stowe's celebrated abolitionist novel *Uncle Tom's Cabin*, along with an edition of Joel Chandler Harris's Uncle Remus stories. In 1898 he published two companion books of his own, *Comical Coons* and *A Coon Alphabet*, both of which abound with drawings of bestial mammy figures, lanky and shiftless Uncle Toms, and knock-kneed children with oversized features wearing ragged clothing, brutalized in physically degrading situations, their English rendered in mocking stereotype, all clearly intended to be read as humorous by white readers. Williams-Forson notes that these images 'provided pleasure at seeing the black child, man, or woman in a compromising position or in one that would seem less threatening to white America's already shaken sense of order and hierarchy'.[22] One such scenario in *Comical Coons*, 'The Coon Skin Cap', features a nervous African American boy wearing the iconic headwear and confronted by a crowd of distraught raccoons who ask, 'Where did you get that hat?' A tree stump in the foreground is marked '"Coon Holler" No Two Legged Coons Wanted Here'.[23] The boy's danger is palpable; the reader is left to imagine what grim fate awaits the unfortunate child when the raccoons' initial shock fades.

'Coon cards' – popular postcards for mailing, or smaller collector cards distributed in cigarette packages – further reinforced these notions. The imagery is by now familiar. A primitivist 1889 cigarette card from North Carolina-based W. Duke, Sons & Co. shows a generic 'African' man with broad features, an animal skin draped on his back, and a gold ring around his neck; the shadow on the wall is that of a raccoon, with the implication being that

In the 1888 presidential campaign Republican Benjamin Harrison, grandson of William Henry Harrison, successfully ran for the office in part on the memory of the 1840 Whig electoral victory, and the now-familiar raccoons and log cabin featured in his campaign materials.

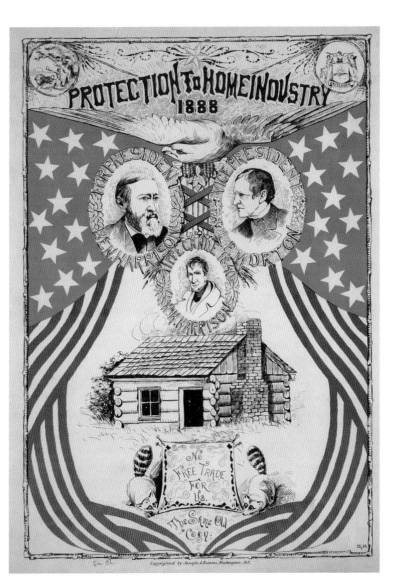

his true self is the 'Coon' from the card's caption. Other images in the fifty-card 'Shadows' series associate Black bodies with sheep, gorillas and fish.

Then there is the logo for the Coon Chicken Inn restaurant chain, founded in 1925 and continuing for twenty years, which featured a grinning and winking Black porter with huge, bright red lips, and 'Coon-Chicken Inn' etched on his oversized teeth, an unsubtle invocation of the stereotype of Black peoples' supposed predilection for eating chicken, and by implication that of the chicken-stealing raccoon and all its burdensome representation. To enter the restaurant, customers walked through an entryway in the shape of the porter's massive open mouth, and within they were served by Black waiters in porter outfits of their own, entirely restricted to the front of the house. Items emblazoned with the logo included dishes, cutlery, children's toys, menu, matchsticks, and even spare tyre covers for advertising around the city.[24] In Seattle, Black citizens actively objected to the restaurant and its ugly imagery, and included organized protests and lawsuits among their responses until the chain shut its doors in the 1950s.

As Jim Crow politics became more deeply entrenched and formalized in law as well as social custom, and as Black activism for civil rights was met by growing white supremacist violence, white representations of Blackness grew ever more exaggerated and malicious. And here is where the racist link between raccoons and coons reaches its most extreme. In the late nineteenth century and well into the twentieth, as the Ku Klux Klan began to gain national notoriety for its 'night rides' involving terrorizing Black families, burning homes, businesses and churches, and lynching, Klansmen found a new euphemism to veil their true intent from outsiders while simultaneously signalling their purpose to sympathetic whites: 'coon hunts'.

The symbolic parallel of the frightened raccoon being harried and treed by a pack of hounds at night with that of a Black person subjected to nocturnal lynch mob violence was not lost on its audiences of whatever race. The mingled mockery and menace were clear, for there was one almost certain gruesome end to both coon hunt and lynching. In his book *Burglar in the Treetops* (1952), a study of game mammals and hunting culture, white Connecticut writer George Heinold offered this casual aside, highlighting what was, to many of his white contemporaries, the wholly unremarkable link between the two bloody activities: 'I vividly remember one coon hunt during my boyhood years. It had the feverish excitement of a lynching party, with the whole community involved.'[25]

The language of commonplace violence against raccoons was a ready surrogate for referencing white violence against African Americans. During a desegregation protest in 1963 a white teen shot and injured four Black civil rights activists in St Augustine, Florida. When arrested, he pleaded not guilty with the wink-and-nod claim that he wasn't shooting at the men but rather firing buckshot 'at a coon over on the beach'. This transparent falsehood was an adequate enough defence for the white judge to release him.[26] Even among these examples, perhaps the most viscerally appalling are lynching photographs, popular souvenirs in white America for the first half of the twentieth century. Typically featuring burned and mutilated Black bodies hanging above a smiling white mob posing proudly for the camera, the photos sometimes featured captions such as 'coon cooking' or 'barbecue'.[27]

While indelibly linked with racism against African Americans, variations on coon have been applied to other communities as well. Cajuns in Louisiana and Texas are sometimes referred to as 'coonasses', derived from either 'the standard French word *conasse*, meaning a stupid person, a bungling prostitute, or an unhealthy prostitute', or 'as a play on the epithet "coon" that alludes to the alleged "racial impurity" of Cajuns or portrays them as lower in status than African Americans'. The stereotype of the bayou-dwelling Cajun who subsists on alligator, possum and raccoon meat is no doubt part of the larger 'coonass' context. It remains a vexed term, proudly claimed by some Cajuns while despised by others; its ironic and even playful use internally among Cajuns is certainly more tolerated than when employed by non-Cajuns, where its use is widely considered a degrading slur.[28]

'Coon' as a racial reference has also been transported from its U.S. zoological, political and social roots and is now part of the white insult lexicon across the British Commonwealth. In Canada, the UK, South Africa, Aotearoa/New Zealand and Australia, 'coon' has regionally specific meanings that differ in significant ways from those of the U.S. For example, the historian T. J. Tallie has analysed the ways that the deposed Zulu king Cetshwayo kaMpande was represented by the British media during his restoration campaign in the 1880s, which included familiar racist minstrel tropes used against the king within the particular political, diplomatic and military concerns of the time. Yet such images were also detached to some degree from the constellation of influences and anxieties that marked the representational particularities of Black subjugation in the U.S., and this made them both more readily appropriated and more unstable in their function. As a result, changing politics on the ground in Natal (current-day KwaZulu-Natal in eastern South Africa) made it possible for Cetshwayo to shift white public perception of his own Blackness in Britain as well as Zulu political autonomy in relation to British imperialism and led to that government's support for his short-lived restoration in 1883.[29]

Similarly, while for much of its history the Cape Minstrel Carnival (Kaapse Klopse) in Cape Town was known as the Coon

RACCOON

This raccoon joins dozens of other animals from around the world in atmospheric lithograph cards advertising the Roulstons Bread company; early 20th century.

Carnival, with its parade of festive and minstrelsy-influenced 'coon troupes', the actual function of 'coon' bears closer scrutiny, for it is not simply a replication of American race relations. The original name of the festival is a clear reference to the coon of imported blackface minstrel performers who first came to Cape Town in 1848, yet minstrel music and later coon songs are only two of many influences on what started as an existing slave holiday, and what since that time have been reinterpreted and integrated through specific local, racial and intercultural dynamics (especially between white, Black and distinctive multi-ethnic (Coloured) populations), and working-class concerns. The Kaapse Klopse is particularly associated with the city's Coloured community and is 'widely held to be a commemoration of the ending of slavery and apprenticeship'.[30] Today, while an ongoing site of ethnic and class contestation, in both imagery and local understanding the festival represents significant differences from the coon of U.S. race relations discussed throughout this chapter.[31]

There is nothing particularly novel in one group of humans using hatred of certain animal species to mobilize violence and degradation against other humans. In all such cases, the animals are doing ideological work for the group in power, and *both* the animal and the humans have to be stripped of value or dignity. Raccoons could only be effective symbols of insult against African Americans once white people had moved them from an honoured category of significance to one of scorn and disregard. Either way, the negative associations that would emerge say almost nothing about either raccoons or African Americans; rather, they tell us a great deal about the racist imagination of those invested in such associations.

To that end, and whatever its contexts and regardless of regional variations, 'coon' represents diverse and vexed concepts connected by a long and often ugly history, with a range of overlapping and competing influences, legacies and meanings. To return to the story about Dr Butler's much-maligned tweet that started this discussion, it is worth observing that white conservative outrage was not so much about how they misunderstood the word's multilayered meaning in African American communities. Rather, through their rigid insistence that the term could *only* have a racist meaning – and that *they*, not Dr Butler or other Black people, were the ones to determine that singular meaning – these critics were firmly reasserting the very ideological power dynamics of white supremacy that have weaponized the term and its associations for so long.

The incident therefore exemplifies the long and painful history of 'coon' and its complex contexts, especially for those human and other-than-human communities most targeted by its violence. Today the word remains just as troublesome as it has been for the past two centuries – entirely appropriate, perhaps, given the complicated representations of its still much-maligned animal namesake.

4 Coonskins and Coon Hunts: The Dead Raccoon

I got one good look
   in the raccoon's eyes
      when he fell from the tree
came to his feet
   and perfectly still
      seized the baying hounds
in his dull fierce glare,
   in that recognition all
      decision lost,
choice irrelevant, before the
   battle fell
      and the unwinding
of his little knot of time began . . .
A. R. Ammons, 'Coon Song'[1]

What does a dead raccoon mean? Raccoons have long been dynamic symbols, and this is as much the case with dead raccoons as their living counterparts. There are arguably more dead raccoons than living ones in the representational archive, and whether employed by poets, film-makers, novelists or comic strip artists, or realized through the fur trade, fashion industry or night-time hunt, the dead, dying or mortally imperilled raccoon crosses forms, genres and media in powerful and often troubling ways. This chapter considers the raccoon as death symbol, and how three iconic images associated in some way with dead raccoons – the coonskin cap, the raccoon skin coat and the coon hunt – offer insight not only into our relationships with the animal itself, but with one another.

Dead raccoons are often invoked as part of a larger meditation on human mortality and the passing of time. Indeed, this linkage

Dead raccoons carry weighty symbolic significance all their own, often gesturing to nature's cycles of birth, growth and decay, as in Kimberly Witham's evocative *On Ripeness and Rot #10 (Raccoon)*.

is so frequent that we might consider raccoons as something akin to secular psychopomps, guides not to an otherworld of the dead but through the existential encounter with our own fleeting life-spans. The raccoon's hybrid melding of human and animal makes it a compelling conductor in this way, for it is both very much like us while remaining entirely Other, in the nebulous border between wild and domesticated, unique and commonplace, a seasoned traveller in all worlds but belonging wholly to none. The raccoon psychopomp may also help reconcile us to our own inevitable demise as more fully part of the natural order.

Even in death, raccoons can be evocative, as in a memorable 1987 Calvin and Hobbes storyline where six-year-old Calvin encounters mortality for the first time when he and his stuffed tiger companion, Hobbes, find an injured raccoon that later dies. While the series mostly focuses on Calvin's hyperactive imagination and the humorous trouble that results, this particular nine-strip theme is an uncharacteristically sombre and understated reflection on the loss of innocence that accompanies each person's realization of their own eventual demise. The animal is gestured to and its presence is powerfully felt, but it remains unseen, perhaps indicative of the ultimate unrepresentability of death.

Most of the time, however, raccoons are marked by their over-determined physical embodiment rather than absence. This is no more the case than in the corporeal remains of the flayed raccoon – or, more colloquially, coonskin, and the popular caps and coats made from their pelt. Fluctuating in demand and desirability, the garments represent many things, not the least being death for millions of raccoons at the whim of capricious markets and unpredictable fashion tastes. One of the most enduring symbols of the U.S. frontier, the coonskin cap has a long and often unclear history, equal parts fact and folklore. White frontiersmen in Kentucky and Tennessee took their common raccoon-skin

Among the more unusual raccoons in Victorian imagery is this plate designed by Theodore Russell Davis *c.* 1880–87 for the state dinner service of U.S. President Rutherford B. Hayes, in which a somewhat spectral raccoon watches a farmer undertake an autumn cornfield burn. Porcelain with chromolithograph, enamel, and gilt decoration.

hunting hats as an essential part of their own patriotic garb – a fashion choice that became magnified in the American nation-building mythology that followed. Later, during the U.S. Civil War, when volunteer companies were called to support the Confederacy, the 'Raccoon Roughs' (pronounced 'rogues') from Tennessee, Alabama and Georgia invoked the earthy pluck and frontier mythos through these distinctive coonskin hats, which were immediately recognizable in muster and on the battlefield.

Yet as a symbol the coonskin cap is more anachronistic nationalist fantasy than historical reality. Although contemporary illustrations would lead us to believe otherwise, the celebrated U.S. personalities Benjamin Franklin, Daniel Boone and William Clark (of Lewis and Clark fame) likely did not wear coonskin caps; even in their own times coonskin was considered common or even undignified for men of means and ambition. Franklin wore a warm fur hat rather than a powdered wig while he was the U.S. representative to France, but it was likely a luxurious fur like sable; according to Boone's own son, the frontiersman explictly chafed at the cap's rustic associations and took offence to depictions of him wearing coonskin. While Clark is often depicted on film and in illustrations as wearing a coonskin cap on his famous journey from 1804 to 1806 exploring the territory claimed by the U.S. in the Louisiana Purchase, there is no evidence to support the folklore; he more likely wore the French-inspired chapeau de bras, which was standard issue uniform for the U.S. Army of the time, or, in colder weather, a more substantial fur hat of lynx, otter or mountain sheep.[2]

The 'right smart coon' Davy Crockett remains the historical figure most widely associated today with raccoons through the

Six-year-old Calvin and his stuffed tiger playmate, Hobbes, philosophize on life and death after finding a mortally injured raccoon.

Drawing of a U.S. Civil War-era uniform from Major General John B. Gordon's 'Raccoon Roughs' mountaineer company.

coonskin cap he supposedly wore, which was itself imbued with frontier significance. His prominence in the Whig Party – which, as we have seen, came to be represented by the raccoon in the 1840s – likely helped fix the association. Once again, it is the Crockett of myth, not fact, who inherited the coonskin mantle. According to the textile and apparel scholar Mitchell D. Strauss, while the coonskin cap was not worn by Crockett as part of his standard attire, he adapted it to augment his legendary status following James Kirke Paulding's *The Lion of the West*, a play in which the 'Crockett' character wore the furry cap. Ironically the play was a satire lampooning Crockett's frontier mythology.[3]

Yet it was not until some decades after his death that Crockett's 'image modulated into respectability when, as the wilderness receded and the myth of the American hunter took hold, his

President Theodore Roosevelt embodies Davy Crockett's wily coon hunter legend in international diplomacy in this cartoon by Charles L. Bartholomew.

OUR MODERN DAVY CROCKETT.

The Coon—Hello, they've given you the gun have they—Well I might as well come down.

From the Minneapolis Journal, Dec. 23 '02

THE TARIFF—DON'T SHOOT, BILL, I'LL COME DOWN!

From The Minneapolis Journal.   Friday, March 5, 1909.

In another Bartholomew cartoon Theodore Roosevelt's presidential successor, the urbane and Yale-educated William Howard Taft, is rendered in iconic frontier buckskin and coonskin cap for his political campaign against trade tariffs.

backwoods persona was converted into the chivalrous hero of stage melodrama' – a persona given renewed life a full century later by Walt Disney.[4]

In Crockett's time as well as ours, the coonskin cap is so firmly linked to a specific kind of idealized wilderness Americanism that it remains inextricably tied to his legacy. Even as celebrated an artist as Pennsylvania's Andrew Wyeth (1917–2009) would find some of his most striking work shadowed by Crockett's oversized

Andrew Wyeth, *Faraway*, 1952, drybrush tempera on panel.

image. Widely recognized for his realist watercolour and tempera works that often focused on spare, pensive rural landscapes and sombre portraits, Wyeth's *Faraway* (1952) is a portrait of his son, Jamie, who sits in the dry grass of a late autumn or winter field, bundled in a thick coat with his arms hugging his knees, pondering the viewer with a pensive, almost sorrowful gaze. On his head, almost covering his right eye, sits a bushy coonskin cap, out of proportion to the boy but somehow appropriate to the scene. While painted a few years before the coonskin cap craze of Disney's Davy Crockett, the painting captured something strangely melancholic that would be lost to many later viewers who carried the more kitschy, popular coonskin associations.

Crockett remains Tennessee's favourite son, and the raccoon stands strong as an emblem of his mythic status in the region, so much so that, in the 1950s, Tennessee senator Estes Kefauver hit the campaign trail in a coonskin cap, invoking Davy's frontier spirit and eliciting grassroots support and establishment scorn in equal measure. He was featured in the trademark cap on the cover of *Time* magazine in 1952, and made campaign appearances with two raccoons named, predictably, Davy Crockett and Daniel Boone. In part because of Crockett's famed association with the animal, in the legislative session of 1971–2 the State of Tennessee made the raccoon the official state animal.

Raccoon skin has not solely been associated with Crockett's world-famous headwear. Indeed, it was as the source of much-in-demand fashion-forward coats in the early twentieth century that the most extensive slaughter of raccoons occurred, resulting in what is to date the species' population nadir.[5] As urbanization and incomes increased throughout the u.s. after the First World War, and as a growing multiracial middle class fuelled demand for luxury items once limited to the rich, the full-length raccoon coat became firmly linked with elite white college culture of the Jazz Age. No longer the rustic 'coonskin' of a previous generation, by 1928 raccoon fur was so fully emblematic of Ivy League life that it became something of an in-joke for critics and aspirants alike.

While cheaper than the more high-end mink, seal and sable fur garments found in the closets of America's wealthy, raccoon coats were still out of reach for most of the country, even in the more affluent 1920s, with prices ranging from $350 to $500, the equivalent of $5,000 today.[6] (For perspective, in 1928 the annual university tuition at Harvard, Yale and Dartmouth was $400.[7]) But for growing numbers of middle-class white collegians eager both to fit in and flout convention among their elite peers, the raccoon coat was an accessible and much-prized accessory that immediately marked one's status in the fashionable set.

Depending on the coat's length and quality of fur, anywhere from 13 to 25 raccoon skins were used for each coat; this did not include the fur used for trimming other garments. While fur sales numbers are difficult to find for this period, and while not all would have been killed for this one garment, it is certainly fair to say that millions of raccoons were killed for this fashion craze, and this calculation is consistent with the documented low point for raccoon numbers in North America.[8]

In the 1920s, raccoon coats were part of a larger generational challenge to the social values of the mouldering Victorian era and the aftermath of the Great War through fashion, literature, music and dance. Alongside faster and more affordable cars, jazz music

Mary La Follette, fashionable daughter of Wisconsin senator Robert M. La Follette Sr, in a full-length raccoon-skin coat, Washington, DC, 1924.

and its emerging interracial exchanges, and flaunting of sexual freedom (especially for women), the raccoon coat was derided by more conservative and largely white commentators as an absurd, vain and even dangerously antisocial symbol of youth rebellion, not to mention the social-climbing ambitions of gauche undesirables.[9] In 1928 a popular dance song by Raymond Klages and J. Fred Coots titled 'Doin' the Raccoon' highlighted the ambivalent democratization represented by the raccoon coat, offering a jaunty, if slightly acidic, commentary on the mixing of social ranks and the absurd pretense of the middle and lower classes acting like upper-class collegians.[10] The song also addresses the popularity of the raccoon coat among so-called 'Hallroom boys', a sly reference to a 1920s comic strip by the Canadian cartoonist Harold MacGill, 'The Hall-room Boys', which featured a couple of scheming young white men whose various attempts to ascend the social ladder and leave their inadequate boarding house lodgings – their 'hall-room' – are constantly thwarted by their own incompetence, bad luck and greed. In spite of the song's jaunty rhythm and what seems to have been a rather vigorous associated dance, its lyrics reveal suspicion about those young men who 'do the Raccoon': are they true Ivy League blue-bloods having fun with their legitimate social peers, or uncouth hall-room grifters trying to rise above their station by putting on airs along with their raccoon coats?

As its popularity expanded, the raccoon coat received substantial ink in the press, some playful, but much derisive. It was featured on the covers of popular magazines like the *Saturday Evening Post* and the *American Magazine*, and received intense attention in Hollywood gossip columns and fan magazines. Even at its best the raccoon coat was seen as useful if frivolous and undignified – fine for the fun-loving, even addle-pated, Ivy League collegiate before the transition to responsible adulthood, useful for warmth in the open motor car at high speeds, but hardly suitable for those with longer-term ambitions for social respectability.

The Great Depression and retrenchment of reactionary social values in the lead-up to the Second World War diminished the raccoon coat craze, and by the late 1930s the familiar association of raccoon fur with rustic foolishness had returned. Now a raccoon coat was singularly a sign of gauche and pathetic pretension, of trying (and failing) to rise above one's station – not unlike the stereotypes that accompanied the nineteenth-century Black dandy in the Zip Coon stereotype.

This is hardly coincidental, for as African Americans and Jews also took to WASP-dominated Ivy League fashion during a period when legal segregation was still firmly embedded in much of American life, its desirability to the latter markedly declined. Even so, the raccoon coat maintained cultural capital in Black and Jewish registers of signification for some time more, independent of the judgements of privileged whiteness. One prominent example is the 1932 photograph 'Couple in Raccoon Coats' by New York photographer James Van Der Zee. A now-iconic image of Black sophistication in urban Harlem, the photo features a stylish African American couple, each draped in an ankle-length raccoon-skin coat, posing on the street with their gleaming limited-edition Cadillac V-16. Historian Jennifer Le Zotte notes that, in Van Der Zee's photograph, the couple 'symbolized the attainment of prosperity for some urban blacks', a far cry from the degrading Jim Crow stereotypes in circulation at the time.[11]

The raccoon coat had a brief resurgence in national popularity in the 1950s with Disney's Davy Crockett, when many surviving Jazz Age garments were profitably recycled as coonskin caps. Otherwise, coonskin's heyday had ended; changing fashions and economics, as well as more widespread anti-fur sentiment,

The influential African American surrealist, jazz poet and musician Ted Joans in his New York studio, 1959. By this period the symbolism of the raccoon coat crossed cultural, economic and ideological boundaries and carried diverse and often competing meanings, but it was also a durable garment of accessible warmth as well as ironic style.

signalled the long decline of raccoon pelts in all but very specialized, ironic or kitschy coonskin contexts.

In the previous chapter we briefly considered the racialized representation of coon hunting, especially in the u.s. Here we build on that discussion to consider the coon hunt as a more specific social practice, in which the threat of the animal's potential death carries as much significance as the end itself. In modern competition hunts, raccoons are treed and left alive, with the purpose of testing the hounds' treeing skills; in the traditional hunts considered here, the intended end is the animal's death, for fur, food, recreation or 'pest' control. In all cases, the raccoons who evade death often assume legendary status among their hunters. These fortunate few are accorded respect based on how often they are able to escape capture. Yet for every raccoon who survives a

In a 2005 performance as 'his alter ego, the shape-shifting, time-travelling, gender-fluid Miss Chief Eagle Testickle', Swampy Cree artist Kent Monkman wore a repurposed raccoon hat as a glam jockstrap, a provocative and playful refusal of settler romanticism that reclaimed the often-despised raccoon as an unexpected object of beauty.

Raccoons from *The Viviparous Quadrupeds of North America*, vol. II (1851), by John James Audubon and John Bachman, hand-coloured lithograph.

traditional coon hunt, countless others die. In 1841 the famed naturalist and artist John James Audubon described a Kentucky coon hunt:

> The racoon [*sic*] was all but swimming, and yet had hold of the bottom of the pool with his feet. The glare of the lighted torch was doubtless distressing to him, his coat was ruffled, and his rounded tail seemed thrice its ordinary size, his eyes shone like emeralds; with foaming jaws he watched the dogs, ready to seize each by the snout if it came within reach. They kept him busy for several minutes; the water became thick with mud; his coat now hung dripping, and his dragged tail lay floating on the surface. His guttural growlings, in place of intimidating his assailants, excited them the more; and they very unceremoniously closed upon him, curs as they were, and without the breeding of gentle dogs! One seized him by the rump and tugged, but was soon forced to let go; another stuck to his side, but soon taking a better directed bite of his muzzle than another dog

had just done of his tail, coon made him yelp, and pitiful were the cries of luckless Tyke. The racoon would not let him go, but in the meantime the other dogs seized him fast, and worried him to death, yet to the last he held by his antagonist's snout. Knocked on the head by an axe, he lay gasping his last breath, and the heaving of his chest was painful to see . . . It was a good scene for a skilful painter.

This is only one of seven raccoon deaths from that single night's hunt, which Audubon chronicles with similar enthusiasm. He concludes as such: 'His fur is good in winter, and many think his flesh good also; but for my part I prefer a live racoon [*sic*] to a dead one, and should find more pleasure in hunting one than in eating him.'[12]

The goals of the coon hunt are diverse: social bonding and entertainment, testing the quality of one's hounds against a small but determined foe, or simply the pursuit of the raccoon, often to a deadly end but sometimes to a nonlethal truce. As a symbol and as a practice, the coon hunt still has deep rural roots, as scholar of hunting culture Wiley Prewitt observes:

In the South, night hunting for possums and coons has long been an important feature of rural life. The fact that possums and coons can survive in settled farming areas has made them available quarry for the poorest hunters. The animals provided rich high-calorie meat and useful, sometimes valuable, hides. And while hunters valued possums mainly as food, they respected coons as worthy game animals. A distinct hunting culture quickly evolved around coons – a culture that centered on the hounds that made the chase possible.[13]

While associated today with the American South, coon hunting was historically widespread in the U.S. east and Midwest, as well as eastern Canada. Indeed, European travellers to these regions remarked on the coon hunt's festive air, and upper-class British commentators found it an interesting counterpart to their own fox hunt. Yet the historian Nicholas W. Proctor notes that they also brought their own class and cultural biases about the proper hierarchy of game animals:

> Such gradations of game became more prevalent through-out the antebellum era. Writing in the mid-1840s, English naturalist Charles Lyell wrote that although he considered raccoon and opossum meat 'too course and greasy for the

'Hunting Opossums and Raccoons', engraving from *Frank Leslie's Popular Monthly* (1878).

palate of a white man . . . the negroes relish them much'
. . . By the end of the antebellum era, few whites would
openly disagree with the South Carolina sportsman who
declared that he considered raccoons and opossums
'vermin too ignoble for the gun', properly hunted only
with 'clubs and curs'.[14]

And this attitude was not only European. In *The Hunter-naturalist:
The Romance of Sporting; or, Wild Scenes and Wild Hunters* (1859),
the Kentucky adventure writer Charles Wilkins Webber describes
a coon hunt with luridly racist prose that vacillates between
patronizing mockery and ugly racial caricature. While hunting
deer and other big game is both acceptable and expected of white
men of a certain station, for a white sportsman to hunt the by
now inherently degraded raccoon is, for Webber, to demean one-
self. The only possible reason to do so is as a socially dangerous

After brining a
raccoon carcass
overnight in a
salt and vinegar
solution, Billy
Washington of
Blue Springs,
Missouri, prepares
it for cooking.
While less
common a source
of animal protein
than in the past,
raccoon continues
to find favour
with wild game
aficionados.

lark that allows one to feel racially superior to the Black men doing the labour of the hunt, but even that is perhaps too much. As game quarry, as in so many ways, raccoons are again mobilized under white supremacy to communicate a diverse range of cultural, class and social meanings.

As a protein source, raccoon meat has long had detractors among wild game enthusiasts, but its partisans praise its gastronomic possibilities. Writing a generation earlier than his fellow English traveller Lyell quoted above, and seemingly without his countryman's racialized aversion to eating raccoon, Arthur Middleton stated that 'its flesh is good eating', but added the wistful caveat 'when we could get nothing else for dinner'.[15] The American writer Mark Twain was a notable fan of raccoon, listing it among the American foods he longed for when on a sojourn in Europe, along with possum, frogs, Philadelphia terrapin soup and pumpkin pie.[16] Today its continuing multiracial consumption is a matter of family and even community pride. In Gillett, Arkansas, an annual 'Coon Supper' has raised funds for local high school students since the 1940s, with hundreds of pounds of raccoon meat cooked every year.[17] As part of his study of Twain's culinary interests, writer Andrew Beahrs offered a vivid description of the Supper's behind-the-scenes process, coming away a somewhat unenthusiastic convert given the extensive bloodletting, grease draining, meat boiling and fat trimming he observed.

Recipes for stewed, boiled, barbecued, brined and roasted raccoon are readily available in print cookbooks and on the Internet, although many of these, too, are fascinating cultural records of changing tastes: for example, the 1975 *Joy of Cooking* included a recipe for sweet potato- and apple-stuffed raccoon, but my own well-worn 1997 revised and updated edition does not include raccoon among the few referenced wild game. While raccoons may now be widespread, consuming them is not. Grammy

Award-winning blues musician Dr. John has a raccoon stew recipe online that features an array of complementary ingredients, including garlic, mirlitons (or chayote, a relative of the gourd family), sweet peppers and vegetable juice. He does, however, caution cooks to be sure to 'skim the oil from the top' after a couple of hours of simmering.[18] By most reports raccoon fat tends to be very strong in smell and flavour; as Beahrs firmly declares, 'Raccoon fat is pretty awful stuff.'[19] But raccoon remains a cherished food for many, across class, racial and generational strata, especially in the American South.

For many Americans there is still a romance to the coon hunt, a nostalgic appeal to a seemingly simpler time. The young-adult novel *Where the Red Fern Grows* (1961) offers insight into that nostalgia and its fracture points. Among the most beloved coming-of-age stories for American youth, the novel by Cherokee Nation writer Wilson Rawls has more than 7 million copies in print, two movie adaptations, and is the inspiration for an annual themed festival and coon hunt in Tahlequah, Oklahoma, capital of the Cherokee Nation, where the novel takes place.

The story focuses on an impoverished but determined boy, Billy Colman, who wants nothing more in the world than a couple of coon-hunting hounds. With a bit of luck and the help of his grandfather, Billy ends up with two Redbone coonhound pups that he names Old Dan and Little Ann, and the story follows their adventures as the boy and his dogs grow up alongside each other in the hill country of northeast Oklahoma. (While Rawls notes explictly that Billy is of mixed Cherokee heritage, illustrators and film-makers have largely emphasized his whiteness.) Multiple generic raccoons die in the dogs' training and the hunting, but the most significant raccoon presence is the 'ghost coon', a shrewd and singular old beast who has never been taken, even when treed by formidable hounds. When the bullying Pritchard boys impugn his dogs' hunting prowess, Billy takes them up on their challenge that Dan and Ann cannot tree the ghost coon. After a dangerous hunt, Billy's hounds manage the supposedly impossible, and he climbs up a tree to knock the raccoon to the hounds below. Here the narrative takes a turn:

> About halfway up, far out on a limb, I found the ghost coon. As I started toward him, my dogs stopped bawling. I heard something I had heard many times. The sound was like the cry of a small baby. It was the cry of a ringtail coon when he knows it is the end of the trail. I never liked to hear this cry, but it was all in the game, the hunter and the hunted.

One of the most celebrated hunting dogs in the United States, the determined, scent-tracking Redbone Coonhound is in part descended from Scottish foxhounds. Its treeing talents pictured here are celebrated in Wilson Rawls's 1961 novel *Where the Red Fern Grows*.

As I sat there on the limb, looking at the old fellow, he cried again. Something came over me. I didn't want to kill him.[20]

After Billy descends, the most sadistic of the Pritchard boys, Rubin, begins beating him for his seeming lack of courage, while Old Dan and Little Ann take on the Pritchards' own vicious hound. In the resulting melee, Rubin runs towards the dogfight with an axe but falls and is mortally injured, while his brother flees in terror. As Billy prepares to leave the deadly scene, he looks up in the tree:

I could see the bright eyes of the ghost coon. Everything that had happened on this terrible night was because of his very existence, but it wasn't his fault.

I also knew he was a silent witness to the horrible scene. Behind me lay the still body of a young boy. On my left a blue tick hound lay torn and bleeding. Even after all that had happened, I could feel no hatred for the ghost coon and was not sorry I had let him live.[21]

The moment of sympathy for the ghost coon is a turning point in the novel, and its cry reverberates through the remainder of the story; after that point, the bloody business of the hunt takes a toll on Billy and his life. First, his grandfather is gravely injured while hunting, then Old Dan is disembowelled by a mountain lion, followed in death shortly thereafter by the heartbroken Little Ann. Yet it is the dogs, not the numerous raccoon corpses strewn throughout the book, whose deaths elicit authorial and audience sympathy. The raccoons are a means to a sad but enlightened end, in large part the motivators and facilitators of Billy's relationship with his hounds.

Not all coon hunt stories are so weighty; some use the hunt for humour and social commentary. During his nearly three-decade career, stand-up comedian Jerry Clower was one of the most recognizable southern entertainers in the U.S. A big, boisterous man with a thick Mississippi accent, his trademark was a lovingly rendered storytelling style rooted in the situational comedy of his rural southern upbringing. One such story by the self-styled 'racoonteur', and his biggest hit, was 'A Coon-huntin' Story' of 1971, a tongue-in-cheek tale of a coon hunt that goes hilariously awry when he and a group of hunters and hounds inadvertently tree a lynx instead of the expected raccoon. John Eubanks, famed throughout the region for his raccoon-hunting prowess, climbs up to knock the canopy-hidden beast down to

Unnamed raccoon hunter with a wall of raccoon pelts and the fundamental tools of his successful trade: an alert hound, a shotgun, and a lantern for night hunting, 1915.

A human feeds bread to a raccoon, 2010.

the dogs only to learn too late of his mistake. The rest of the story entails the unsuspecting men on the ground crying out 'Knock him out, John!' while John screams, 'This thing's killing me!' and begs his employer, Mr Baron, to shoot the animal in the canopy as it mauls him. When Baron demurs, fearful of striking the unseen John, the latter cries out, 'Well just shoot up in here amongst us – one of us got to have some relief!'[22] The story ends in the audience's laughter without resolution for John, the lynx or the hunters. It is easy to forget that the story began with four raccoons killed earlier in the hunt, now entirely an afterthought.

The coon hunt has four essential characteristics: a raccoon, a night-time rural setting (often a wooded or swampy habitat), human hunters and, most importantly, one or more coonhounds. The raccoon is a variable that may or may not be found on the night, but the coonhounds are carefully considered, and a good hound is a point of pride for any hunter:

> Though determining pedigree is a risky task, most coon-
> dog breeds probably evolved from hounds brought from
> Europe during colonial times, combined with countless

intentional and unintentional matings with other canines. Early hunters certainly bred more for hunting ability than for breed type. Nowadays, the black and tan, the redbone, the bluetick, the English, the treeing Walker, and the Plott are among the standard breeds that hunters say can potentially make good coon hounds. Coming from a recognized breed, however, does not guarantee that the dog will prove itself on game. A hound that runs only coons (that is, a 'straight' coon dog), or even one that runs *mostly* coons, is always greatly prized among hunters.[23]

A good coonhound is not just a good physical tracker but one that calls well – the plaintive, bellowing 'song' of a coonhound is, according to many hunters, as much a practical attribute as a deeply pleasing sound, and skilled hunters can readily recognize the specific calls of individual dogs on the hunt, as well as whether those dogs are lost, trailing quarry or have treed a raccoon.

Descended from a wide range of hunting hounds, including bloodhounds and foxhounds, the Black and Tans were the first coonhounds to be recognized by the American Kennel Club in 1945.[24] Both the raccoon-associated Davy Crockett and Daniel Boone have been cited as having kennels from which today's coonhound breeds are descended, although how much of that is mythology and how much is fact is debatable. Like coonskin caps, coonhounds represent far more than just attractive dogs with impressive hunting abilities; to their partisans they are 'distinctively American', as the outdoorsman and writer-editor Warren H. Miller proudly declared in 1919, and have 'had as much to do with the development of our country as the pioneer himself'.[25] And while the wily raccoon may be Tennessee's official state animal, the mascot of the state's flagship university is Smokey, the raccoon's relentless coonhound nemesis.

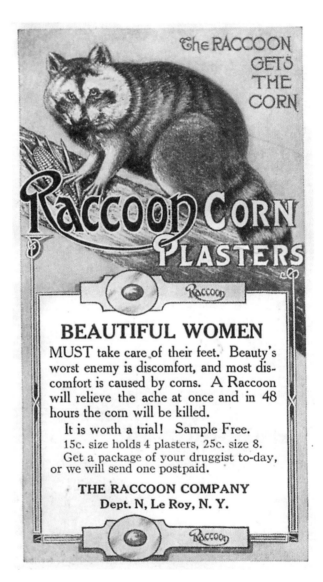

The long historical association of raccoons with maize – 'corn' – is a rather heavy-handed marketing conceit in this corn plaster advertisement from the early 1900s.

5 Rascals and Rockets: Raccoons in Popular Culture

What do you want? I whisper to the raccoon in my sleep.
  What do you want?
'What do you want?' the raccoon whispers back. *'What
  do you want?'*
Gregory Blake Smith, 'Hands'[1]

Whether the stuff of dreams or nightmares, raccoons in the human imagination have a lot to whisper about our individual and collective relationships to the wild world, but raccoons in oral and ceremonial traditions and various literary and visual arts are only part of this representational archive. We now make a brief sojourn into raccoons in popular culture: on film and television, in comics on screen and page, and in diverse other forms, such as marketing, video games, heraldry and sport. Some are very familiar outlaws and rogues; others offer more unique qualities for consideration. All, however, affirm the continued human fascination with raccoons living and dead alike.

Memorable raccoon characters with distinctive personalities are relatively scarce in film; they most often serve gory, ironic or comic effect in demonstrating the danger of human hubris towards the natural world. Sometimes raccoons are resistance fighters or sly opportunists, such as Bruce Willis's roguish RJ in the animated film *Over the Hedge* (2006), the story of a raccoon who, in trying to manipulate a group of suburban animals to help him pay off his food debt to an angry bear, ends up thwarting an extermination campaign led by the officious chair of the human homeowners' association; a more menacing and Machiavellian raccoon ringleader was voiced by Liam Neeson in *The Nut Job*

George Ethelbert Walsh was among many early 20th-century writers whose romanticized depictions of wildlife drew the scorn of more ostensibly scientific nature observers like Theodore Roosevelt and John Burroughs. In *Washer the Raccoon* (1922), the eponymous character is raised by wolves after being separated from his procyonid family; here he waves farewell to his lupine foster mother. Colour plate by Edwin John Prittie.

(2014). While the unnamed raccoon in *Furry Vengeance* (2010) leads an animal rebellion against the destruction of their forest home by a real estate developer, it is a very minor high point of an otherwise execrable film starring Brendan Fraser and Brooke Shields. It certainly seems that any movie with a camping theme will have one or more troublemaking raccoons as antagonists to the hapless humans in the wilderness; increasingly we see menacing urban raccoons, too, as in the comedic mauling of the naive human-raised-by-elves Buddy by a New York City raccoon in the surprise Christmas hit *Elf* (2003), starring Will Ferrell.

Of all media corporations, the Walt Disney Company has had the most significant influence on raccoon representation. As wholesome Americana has long been core to the Disney brand and its global marketing, what could be more American than that ever-malleable native raccoon? From the raccoon-garbed Lost Boys twins in *Peter Pan* (1953), the horde of angry raccoons attacking bears Kenai and Koda and their human friend Nita in *Brother Bear 2* (2006) and the determined raccoon battling the superhuman baby Jack-Jack in *The Incredibles 2* (2018), to Davy Crockett's coonskin cap craze in the 1950s and the 1969 'boy and his coon' family film version of Sterling North's influential book *Rascal*, to the troublemaking Meeko in *Pocahontas* (1995) and misanthropic Rocket Raccoon from the Marvel Cinematic Universe (which Disney acquired in 2009), among many others, Walt Disney's namesake company has had an incalculable influence on how generations of viewers perceive these animals. As *Rascal*'s story receives attention elsewhere in the book, we will attend here to Crockett, Meeko and Rocket, who hold much more global familiarity.

For a generation of American television viewers in the 1950s and '60s, Davy Crockett epitomized the nostalgic frontier Americanism then emerging as the Cold War counterpoint to a hyper-industrialized Soviet Union, part of 'a long tradition of national heroes as embodiments of the national character, most in the mold of the great white male' who 'led the American people on their divinely appointed mission into the wilderness and set the cultural standard for the settlements that would follow'.[2] Many Americans looked to both the space age frontier future and, for white Americans in particular, to a mythic frontier past for seemingly uncomplicated narratives of the nation's ostensibly unique destiny.

Hollywood was an integral part of that peculiar self-fashioning, with the patriotic Walt Disney at the forefront of the post-war and Cold War effort. Disney brought his movies to the cause along with the increasingly popular medium of television; ever the businessman, he also used the opportunity to market his new Disneyland theme park. In the October 1954 premiere episode of *Disneyland* – which would quickly become a top weekly television show with tens of millions of viewers – the animated character Tinker Bell introduced the theme park's many themed 'realms' by flying between them in ever-changing costumes. Tink's travels from Frontierland directly to Tomorrowland explicitly link the frontier wilderness of the past to the cosmic frontiers of the future. Disney himself then appears to point out figures from American folklore on a map and describes Frontierland as follows:

Behind the gates of Frontierland is the inspirational America of the past century. Here is the treasure of our native folklore, the songs, tales, and legends of the big men who built the land. Some of them were completely legendary, like Paul Bunyan the woodchopper with his blue ox, Babe. Then again we find that true stories about real people can be fabulous too. Now in our TV series from

Frontierland, we're going to tell about these real people who became legend, like Davy Crockett, our first coonskin congressman.[3]

The camera zooms in on a picture of actor Fess Parker as Crockett in coonskin cap and buckskin, swinging his rifle by the barrel as he fights Mexican soldiers, a scene that would later be the character's off-camera death in the doomed Texas Alamo. From there, the scene moves back in time to a down-home Smoky Mountain-set scene of the countrified Parker singing his show's theme song to the camera.

The commercial impact was immediate. 'Like a sonic boom,' Lisa Anne Fischman observes,

> Disney's Davy Crockett generated seemingly endless waves of frenzied merchandising and wild consumer demand . . . Disney did his best to push the craze along by combining the first televised segments into a feature-length film, *Davy Crockett: King of the Wild Frontier*, for theatrical release in May of 1955.

This was followed by Crockett segments on the *Mickey Mouse Club*, which also premiered that year. The Crockett-centred Frontierland became a runaway marketing brand with toy flint-lock rifles, buckskin, bows and arrows, and other kitschy frontier paraphernalia selling worldwide, but it was the coonskin cap that was the core sales phenomenon. It was so popular that raccoon fur sales went from 25 cents to $8 per pound in the first year alone, with sales of upwards of 10 million officially licensed caps and an untold number of cheap knock-offs.[4]

Disney was certainly correct that 'Davy's life was so fantastic, it's hard to tell where fact left off and fancy began', but not only

While Fess Parker's on-screen portrayals of Davy Crockett and Daniel Boone both featured coonskin caps, there is little evidence that the historical personalities themselves wore the now-iconic headwear. Boone seems to have been particularly hostile to the association, while Crockett largely used coonskin when running for U.S. Congress to firm up his frontier bona fides.

on television. The historical Crockett may well have worn such a hunting cap during his service in the devastating campaign against the Red Stick Creeks under then-General Andrew Jackson in 1812, but he seems to have used it mostly to solidify his image of uncorrupted common man to Tennessee voters before leaving politics to support U.S. expansionist interests in Mexican-claimed Texas, where he would die at the Alamo mission in 1836. (There is no reliable evidence that he wore a coonskin cap in his final battle; Fess Parker and John Wayne both sported coonskin in their 1955 and 1960 filmic death scenes, but Billy Bob Thornton's world-weary 2004 Crockett explicitly eschews it as celebrity artifice before his execution by Mexican troops under command of General Santa Anna.)

Forty years after Parker and Disney turned coonskin into a cultural phenomenon, the Walt Disney Studios hit it big with another prominent raccoon: Meeko, the animal sidekick to the eponymous Powhatan 'princess' in the big-screen animated feature *Pocahontas* (1995) and its 1998 direct-to-TV sequel, *Pocahontas II: Journey to a New World*. In both these films Meeko is firmly in the 'wilderness icon' category of raccoon representation; his natural habitat is the cultivated forest territories of the Powhatan people in seventeenth-century North America, at the dawn of English colonization. The Pocahontas films are *very* loosely based on the historical encounter between the peoples of the Powhatan Confederacy and the Virginia Company of England in Tsenacommacah. The first film follows in the long colonial tradition of romanticizing the largely non-existent interactions

Given that the English word 'raccoon' comes to us directly from the Powhatan *arakun* and the writings of John Smith, the inclusion of Meeko the raccoon as a sidekick character is one of the few legitimate nods to historical or cultural accuracy in Disney's *Pocahontas* (1995).

between Captain John Smith and Pocahontas; the second follows Pocahontas to England, where she becomes embroiled in a love triangle with Smith and the tobacco planter-merchant John Rolfe. (Pamunkey and Mattaponi oral tradition asserts that Pocahontas was a child when she briefly met Smith, that she was later kidnapped by the English and subjected to sexual abuse in their custody, that the English killed her Powhatan husband, and that her 'marriage' to Rolfe was anything but consensual.[5]) In both films, Pocahontas is accompanied by two animal friends native to the Americas: Flit, the feisty ruby-throated hummingbird, and the raccoon Meeko, whose excessive appetite and curiosity lead him into constant conflict with the invading English.[6]

Meeko was not originally planned for the film, at least not as we know him. Pocahontas's primary comic sidekick was initially to be a talkative wild turkey named Redfeather, based on the comedic stylings of John Candy, who may have recorded at least part of the dialogue before his unexpected death in 1994.[7] Around that time, studio executives decided on a more ostensibly realistic approach to the film's animals, having them pantomime but not speak, and Redfeather was cut in favour of Flit and Meeko as dual embodiments of Pocahontas's personality and conscience.[8]

The shift from animal characters with human voices to relative voicelessness undermines the film's foundational ethos of cross-cultural communication. In her signature song 'Colours of the Wind', Pocahontas implores Smith to listen to the animal and elemental voices of her North American homelands, but she herself is unable to speak to her animal companions in their own languages or even in a shared speech. Meeko and Flit clearly understand the human Powhatan language, but they must resort to exaggerated pantomime to communicate ideas to Pocahontas, so it seems that she, like Smith, is similarly limited in her capacity of speaking to the other-than-human world.

Verisimilitude is certainly not a necessary goal of all animated films, yet *Pocahontas* is explicitly based on actual persons and events, widely advertised as being attentive to historical, cultural and zoological realism. If accuracy is put forward as a guiding principle for design and production, it is fair to test the work against its own stated terms. As a problematically revisionist myth of settler redemption and Indigenous decline, *Pocahontas* stumbles far more than it succeeds, at least on the historical front. Regarding zoological accuracy, however, Meeko's distinctive chitter, mischievous personality and character design demonstrate clear familiarity with actual raccoon behaviour and physiology. Even so, his largely utilitarian role as embodied animal conscience undermines Pocahontas's own authority as a moral agent as well as his own, not to mention the deadly seriousness of the Powhatan struggle against the cultural and ecological catastrophes that would accompany English colonization. These are hardly the lessons intended by a film widely viewed by admirers and critics alike as carrying messages of socially progressive environmental activism.[9]

In 2012, nearly twenty years after *Pocahontas* brought Meeko to the screen, Disney's Marvel Studios announced that the long-rumoured *Guardians of the Galaxy* film was in production. The announcement signalled the studio's Phase 2 extension of their cinematic universe into a wider intergalactic setting and thus a more expansive range of characters and storylines from the Marvel archive. Yet many observers were perplexed, as the Guardians were among the most obscure of Marvel's comic book hero ensembles. It also introduced some challenging characters to help carry a major Hollywood film, for among the Guardians to receive substantial screen time were a nearly monosyllabic tree-man named Groot and a surly, gun-toting, 4-foot-tall bipedal raccoon named Rocket.

Rocket Raccoon is a far more complex character to discuss than either Meeko or Davy Crockett, especially given his multiple iterations in comics and video games, on television and in the movies. Rocket has been given life by numerous writers and artists since Bill Mantlo introduced him in *Marvel Preview 7* in 1976, developed his character further with artist Keith Giffen in *The Incredible Hulk* #271 (1982) and gave firm form to his personality and backstory in a miniseries of 1985 with artist Mike Mignola. Rocket is most recognizable to mainstream audiences today in the Marvel Cinematic Universe, especially the *Guardians of the Galaxy* films directed by James Gunn and the two *Avengers* films directed by Anthony and Joe Russo. Voiced to impressive effect by Philadelphia-born American actor Bradley Cooper, the big-screen Rocket is a significant departure from his comic book counterpart.

Mantlo and Mignola's miniseries takes inspiration from a bewildering number of disparate sources, including Disney's *Mary Poppins*, the Keystone Cops slapstick film series of the early twentieth century, u.s. evangelical ministry, the 1962 novel and 1975 film adaptation of Ken Kesey's *One Flew Over the Cuckoo's Nest*, Edgar Allan Poe, frightening circus clowns, and the merciless business practices of 1980s corporate culture. Yet foremost among these, perhaps, is the Beatles' music, especially 'Rocky Raccoon' (1968) and 'I Am The Walrus' (1967), even though neither song is really about the title animals. (The 1976 version of the Marvel character is, in fact, named Rocky, not Rocket, and his exaggerated English accent is a gesture to Lennon's Liverpudlian roots. He has a more ostensibly American accent in Mantlo's second Rocket story, and Cooper turned that into the 'Gilbert Gottfried meets Joe Pesci' mash-up for the Marvel films.[10])

Fans familiar with only the films may be surprised that Rocket's main sidekick before Groot was a cybernetically enhanced pinniped, appropriately (if not imaginatively) named Wal Rus. Rocket, just like the Beatles' Rocky, has an interest in guns, but whereas the latter is a poor marksman and ends up shot by his rival Dan, Rocket is a master with weapons of all kinds. The non-sensical songs by John Lennon and Paul McCartney are playful touchstones for the Mantlo and Mignola story arc, which alter-nates between the frustratingly strange and delightfully bizarre.

In the comics Rocket started life as an ordinary Earth raccoon, brought to the Keystone Quadrant sector of deepest space as part of a psychiatric initiative by the supervisory 'Shrinks' on Half-world, a planetary asylum for the incurably insane designed to protect them from persecution on their home world and, not incidentally, to prevent them from re-entering the broader cosmic society. Halfworld is thus both sanctuary and prison. In the past the Shrinks and their robotic assistants collected animals from Earth and introduced them to the patients (with the cringeworthy name of 'Loonies') as companions and playthings. After many years, the Shrinks departed and left patient care to the robots, who eventually tired of their task and used their technology to modify the animals with advanced intelligence and physical abilities. The task of patient care then shifted to the animals of Halfworld, and the robot overseers undertook other labour, such as weapon, rocketry and toy manufacture. Some of the animals were trained to be Rangers, Halfworld's elite protective security force, and this is Rocket's role at the start of the miniseries. Groot is nowhere to be seen in this early stage, as Rocket's primary companions are his otter girlfriend Lylla and the aforementioned Wal Rus.

This is about as clear a summary as is possible, as the story just gets more convoluted from there, with killer robotic clowns, a mercenary rabbit brigade, bomb-hurling monkeys, the corpor-ate toy company machinations of a malevolent mole mastermind, and a complicated sub-plot surrounding the theft and recovery of the planet's unreadable historical record and psychiatric treatment plan known as Gideon's Bible.

What is relevant here, however, is that Rocket, far from the law-breaking bounty hunter depicted in the films and subsequent comic, game and cartoon versions, starts out as one of Halfworld's most chivalric defenders of justice; he approaches his duties with integrity and treats his mentally ill human charges with kindness and sympathy. As raccoon representations go, Rocket, in each of his iterations, cuts new trail – neither rogue, prey, vermin nor wilderness icon, but rather a courageous spacefaring champion of some of the universe's most vulnerable and misunderstood inhabitants.[11]

While the filmic Rocket is complex and multilayered in his own right, he hews much closer to conventional ideas of raccoon outlawry and lawlessness. A poignant scene in the first *Guardians*

Guardians of the Galaxy director and co-writer James Gunn walks the red carpet with a live raccoon in lieu of the film's computer-generated mercenary, Rocket, at the 2014 European premiere.

film, released in 2014, seems to entirely erase his history of caring for the vulnerable. In a drunken row, the fearsome Drax the Destroyer refers to Rocket as 'vermin', which drives the hypersensitive raccoon into a fury. As the leader of the Guardians, Peter Quill (aka Star-Lord) tries to dissuade him from blasting Drax with his laser cannon, but Rocket's anguish is palpable: 'He thinks I'm some stupid thing – he does! Well, I didn't ask to get made! I didn't ask to be torn apart and put back together over and over, turned into some . . . some little monster.'[12] The scene gestures to an earlier moment when Quill, having just been imprisoned with the soon-to-be Guardians, gets a furtive glimpse as Rocket is putting on his prison uniform and sees scar tissue and metal implants stretching across the raccoon's back. Further, Rocket's Nova Corps criminal record indicates years of antisocial and destructive behaviour, and the films indicate that this is traced directly to his brutal treatment as a laboratory experiment on Halfworld. The movie Rocket is very far indeed from Ranger Rocket, the dedicated protector of the disabled and marginalized; he's now joined their ranks, a hurt and lonely cynic who steals an imprisoned amputee's leg prosthetic for a laugh, but also hungers for friendship.

While more noble and more unique among raccoon representations than the filmic Rocket, the Mantlo and Mignola comic-book Rocket has a far more circumscribed character arc – there is no identifiable growth, and he begins and ends with the same heroic qualities. One of the memorable aspects of Rocket's presentation in the Marvel films is that he is deeply flawed and quite obviously wounded, but also fiercely loyal to those who earn his trust; perhaps this is why Gunn has described Rocket and his origin story as 'the heart' of the first *Guardians* movie:

it's really, really important to me that Rocket Raccoon . . . is not a cartoon character, it's not Bugs Bunny in the middle of *The Avengers*, it's a real, little, somewhat mangled beast that's alone. There's no one else in the universe quite like him, he's been created by these guys to be a mean-ass fighting machine.[13]

Roguish raccoons are far more common in popular culture than are selfless champions, but ne'er-do-wells are often complex characters with clear potential for meaningful change. And Rocket does change: in the Russo Brothers' paired *Avengers* films (*Infinity War* and *Endgame*) that followed Gunn's two *Guardians* movies, Rocket's heroic qualities come fully to the fore, and he emerges from that traumatic, multiverse-spanning epic as something approaching the righteous champion of the early comics. There are decidedly few raccoons in popular culture that manage to connect emotionally with audiences as memorably as this 'mangled', misanthropic 'little monster' with the heart of a hero.

Beyond Rocket, the few prominent raccoon characters from comic strips and books are represented as decidedly living creatures with personalities and motivations all their own, not simply dead or symbolic facilitators of other characters' enlightenment. Firmly in the raccoon trickster vein is RJ, from the syndicated comic strip *Over the Hedge* by T. Lewis and Michael Fry, which inspired the 2006 animated film. A rather different raccoon character is Rackety Coon Chile from Walt Kelly's

A reflective Rackety Coon Chile considers the deeper significance of Memorial Day in Walt Kelly's *Pogo*, 30 May 1955.

long-running *Pogo* newspaper strip (1948–73) that chronicled the lives, friendships and mock-epic politics of anthropomorphic beasts in the Okefenokee Swamp on the boundary of Georgia and Florida. Among the many creatures that call the Okefenokee home alongside the ever-patient protagonist Pogo Possum is the Rackety Coon family: hard-working Ma, moonshining Pa and their wise-beyond-his-years son, Rackety Coon Chile. In the hands of a lesser artist the strip's stereotypical dialect and sharp wordplay would have been condescending, but Kelly's respect for the people, the land and the animals of the American South infused the strip throughout its run, and he explored the vagaries of American political culture with a generosity and sly courage rarely equalled by his contemporaries. While not a major character in the series, Rackety Coon Chile is consistently a voice of good sense and philosophical consideration, and is one of the swamp children least likely to get into major mischief – rather against type for a species so often represented as roguish.

Today it is online that comic strips have found new audiences, and it is there that we find one of the longest-running raccoon comic characters: Woo, from the webcomic *Sandra and Woo*. A collaboration between German writer Oliver Knörzer and Indonesian artist Powree, the series features American middle-school student Sandra North and her pet raccoon, Woo. The series is ostensibly about Sandra's coming-of-age adventures and social

Rascal, the title raccoon from Sterling North's popular novel, casts a long shadow in this humorous metatextual commentary from the long-running online comic strip, *Sandra and Woo*, by Powree and Oliver Knörzer.

struggles, yet Woo's propensity for mischief is often given centre stage. Unique in the characterization of anthropomorphized comic raccoons is the care that Knörzer and Powree bring to Woo's life as an other-than-human being, and readers are regularly treated to well-researched information about raccoon diet, behaviour, breeding, habitat, and cultural and natural history. In addition, Woo and other animals not infrequently face severe injury or death – from humans, predators and mischance – which brings a level of realism and pathos to the otherwise largely humorous narrative. Begun in 2008, as of this writing it is ongoing, with a substantial online archive and a growing fanbase.

Raccoons make their appearances on television, computer and gaming screens, too. An adult Canadian comedy, the live-action *Crawford*, featured a running storyline of raccoons invading a family's home and bringing additional chaos to what was already a challenging family dynamic; those raccoons join more recent animated raccoons for a decidedly adult audience, such as Lifty and Shifty, the larcenous green raccoon brothers in the ultraviolent web series *Happy Tree Friends* (1999–2006), whose antics generally end with their gory dismemberment, or the Batmanesque 'Coon' superhero persona of the foul-mouthed Eric Cartman from *South Park* (a provocative choice that explicitly plays with mainstream audience discomfort around the term 'coon').

For a younger crowd, the most prominent television procyonids feature on *The Raccoons*, an environmentally themed animated children's show, aired in Canadian television specials from 1980 to 1985 and then as a regular series distributed internationally on the Disney Channel and the BBC until 1992. Adventure-loving, bent-nosed Bert Raccoon and his married raccoon roommates, Ralph and Melissa, continually work against the corporate machinations of the cigar-chomping pink aardvark Cyril Sneer, who seeks to turn their peaceful Evergreen Forest home into profitable timber, only to be continually thwarted by the trio and their various woodland friends. Propelled by gentle adventure and a focus on friendship and ethical growth, the series follows a now very familiar association of raccoons with the wild world in its advocacy of environmental stewardship. It also featured top animation and voice talent, including folk singer Rita Coolidge, country music superstar Dottie West and actor-singer John Schneider. While its anthropomorphic characters are a considerable distance from their animal counterparts, *The Raccoons* remains a nostalgic favourite among Canadian viewers of the late 1980s and early 1990s. Yet aside from this series, substantive raccoon characters in children's television are few, and they tend to be side personalities rather than main characters.

Beyond Marvel's Rocket and Disney's Meeko, of all recent pop culture raccoons the most popular would certainly be Sly Cooper,

New York Governor Hugh Carey with skiers and a live raccoon (in lieu of the cartoon mascot Roni) at the 1980 Winter Olympics, Lake Placid, New York.

TM   TM

Ranger Rick Raccoon has been the animal ambassador for the National Wildlife Federation since 1959. Debuting in 1967, NWF's children's magazine, *Ranger Rick*, has provided science-based wildlife information to generations of budding American ecologists and nature lovers.

In the tradition of Smokey Bear and Woodsy Owl, Howdy the Good Outdoor Manners Raccoon was the slightly eerie animal mascot of the Pennsylvania Game Commission and championed 'common sense rules of courtesy and respect that characterize every true sportsman and conservationist'. *Pennsylvania Game News*, June 1959.

the title character of a series of popular Sony PlayStation games released between 2002 and 2013. The four games and various offshoots of the *Sly Cooper* series fully embrace the trope of the outlaw raccoon – indeed, it is central to the game world's story and design. The eponymous character is the last of a long line of high-end raccoon thieves, a family so notorious and so skilled that other animal criminals covet the secrets of their extraordinary powers. Rather than the mercenary and often self-centred filmic Rocket, Sly is a raccoonish Robin Hood dedicated to stealing from the wicked and restoring his family's lost honour. Sadly for raccoon partisans and fans of the franchise, as of this book's printing a series of planned multimedia *Sly Cooper* projects were on hold with little hope of their resurrection.

In closing this discussion, it is worth considering another area of raccoon representation: emblemry, in the form of individual symbols, logos, and corporate and sports mascots. As we might expect, the wilderness associations of raccoons are prominent, so it is no surprise that Ranger Rick Raccoon has served as the 'wildlife ambassador' for the U.S. conservation group the National Wildlife Federation for more than fifty years, and their children's magazine has carried his name since 1967.[14] A decidedly more disturbing animal ambassador is Howdy, the Good Outdoor Manners Raccoon, who educated Pennsylvania nature lovers about socially acceptable behaviour in the great outdoors from 1959 through the 1980s. His genial characteristics of perky ranger's hat, cosy flannel shirt and pudgy tummy are offset by an overly large, bulging stare, slightly vacant smile and well-worn mallet,

For all their economic and symbolic significance, raccoons are a rarity among heraldic beasts. The archives of the UK's College of Arms include only a few raccoons as crest animals. Pictured here are the procyonid arms of D. C. Holmes, C. E. Edgar, C.W.G. Portal-Foster and J.W.H. Silvester.

giving him a somewhat menacing air.[15] The 1980 Winter Olympics in Lake Placid, New York, featured the mascot 'Roni' the Raccoon, its name chosen by New York State students to represent the native animal's history in the region as a gesture to *atí:ron*, the Mohawk word for the species. And London agency Winkreative chose Mr Porter, the dapper raccoon mascot of Toronto-based Porter Airlines, specifically for its iconic significance in order 'to furnish Porter Airlines with a mascot that represented Canada while avoiding the ubiquitous maple leaf. A raccoon was partly chosen for its visual appeal and its reputation as a smart and cheeky creature.'[16]

Given the significance of raccoons to the UK's fur-trade fortunes and those of its colonial descendants, it is curious that there are not more raccoons represented in British heraldry, but the UK's College of Arms has only four or five raccoons in its substantial archives. The animals are similarly rare as sports mascots; as the official animal of Tennessee, the raccoon was a sensible symbolic choice for the Tennessee Titans NFL franchise, although the team's branding emphasizes a blade-like letter 'T' in a red, white and blue fireball rather than T-Rac, their cheerleading raccoon. Far more common than raccoons proper in U.S. high school and university sports mascotry are burly, bearded men wearing coonskin caps, variously invoking the white frontiersmen, pioneers and mountaineers with whom such caps have long been associated, another way in which dead raccoons retain a prominence beyond that of their living counterparts.

OCTOBER 1955   25¢

Field & Stream.

IS PUBLIC HUNTING
DOOMED?

KILLER COON

Beginning A New Serial
THE BIG SAFARI
A Story of Adventure
and Intrigue in Africa

6 Trash Panda: Pet and Pest

> The planters considered them as one of their greatest miseries.
> In a single night a swarm of these creatures would do more
> injuries than the labours of a month could repair. But in a
> state of tameness the raccoon is both harmless and amusing.
> John Tillotson, *Tales about Animals*[1]

The American term 'varmint' is a colloquial form of the more
standardized 'vermin', just as 'critter' is a variant on 'creature'.
'Varmint', or 'vermin', is an ever-contextual category, not unlike
that of the human outlaw with which raccoons are so often associated. As the animal studies scholar Lucinda Cole writes:

> Historically, 'vermin' is a slippery term because it refers
> neither to a particular biological classification nor to a
> group of genetically related animals; instead, it names a
> category of creatures defined according to an often un-
> stable nexus of traits: usually small, always vile, and, in
> large numbers, noxious and even dangerous to agricul-
> tural or sociopolitical orders. The characteristic feature of
> vermin is that they reproduce so rapidly and in such
> numbers they threaten to overwhelm their biological, en-
> vironmental and – from a human perspective – sociolegal
> contexts.[2]

For human and other-than-human outlaws alike, there are often
deadly consequences for lingering too long in that interpretive
borderland.

Yet so many of the animals we consider pests are actually those
adaptive species that flourish in areas where humans presume

Hunter becomes
the hunted: a feral,
anthropomorphized
raccoon attacks
a sad-eyed
coonhound
in Bob Kuhn's
dramatic cover
art for this
sportsmen's
magazine
from 1955.

to dominate: raccoons, certainly, but coyotes, crows, rats and cockroaches, too. Perhaps there is something existentially threatening to us about their ability to turn our homes, habits and ecological impacts to their own advantage. They put the lie to our sense of hominid omnipotence, and we hate and fear them for it, even when we accord some individuals of their kind a measure of tolerance.

For all that raccoons have been understood as honoured anomalies, trickster-teachers and animal companions, their lives have long overlapped with our own, and the resulting conflicts have made them a target of persecution. Frequently killed as pests and problems, raccoons are also prized for their companionship – and not only in North America. But the boundary between pet and pest is a narrow one far too easily transgressed. This chapter consider raccoons in their dual roles as beloved pets and despised vermin.

'Bandits', a bronze fountain sculpture of rubbish-raiding raccoons by the artist Joffa Kerr, stands in Menlo Park, California.

We often think of the relationship between humans and domesticated animals as one infused with benevolent, even noble, intent, but the making of animals into pets is very often an exercise of unrecognized violence not dissimilar from their persecution as vermin. Yi-Fu Tuan makes the provocative argument that the process of pet-making is one intimately (if often invisibly) embedded in inequities of power and authority:

> pets exist for human pleasure and convenience. Fond as owners are of their animals, they do not hesitate to get rid of them when they prove inconvenient . . . When they grow to a size that makes their presence in the house problematical and, above all, when they begin to respond to the imperatives of their sexual nature, the temptation to destroy them increases.[3]

Raccoons as pets are emblematic of this pattern, having often been subject to constant, normalized violence, as Leon F. Whitney and Acil B. Underwood illustrate in their book *The Raccoon* (1952): 'Discipline may be accomplished in several ways. One is to return him to his cage when he misbehaves; another is to box the ears, which in the case of some coons becomes real discipline.' Even though they explicitly acknowledge that a raccoon is 'an extremely quick and sensitive animal' with 'a higher degree of intelligence than any other except the monkey', they do not hesitate to endorse physical abuse to compel obedience – indeed, they encourage it.[4]

As discomfiting as it may be for those of us who live with and claim to love our animal companions, the total domination of their existence *is* the foundation of pet 'ownership', as we decide when and what they eat and how or if they exercise to how they amuse themselves, where and when they sleep, whether they are able to reproduce. And knowing what we do about their curiosity

Most photographs of pet raccoons from the late 19th and early 20th centuries feature chains, a particular torment for such a curious and adventurous animal wholly unsuited to domestication as a pet. Photograph by Harris & Ewing, c. 1913.

and intelligence, there is something indescribably tragic in old photographs of 'tamed' pet raccoons weighed down with heavy chains to prevent them from climbing trees or otherwise exploring their world as both instinct and desire would compel them.

A typical example is Mason A. Walton's memoir *A Hermit's Wild Friends; or, Eighteen Years in the Woods* (1903), which includes a lengthy account about the ill-named 'Satan', the 'artful old coon' he trapped and forced into captivity; his almost wistful recounting of the myriad abuses he inflicted to break the raccoon's defiant spirit is difficult reading today. Here is just one example:

> [Satan] did not take kindly to cage-life, although his cage was under a small pine-tree, so when I was about the cabin I chained him to the tree and let him run outside. I put him in the cage every day before going to the city for my mail. He resented this, and would run up the pine-tree when he saw me lock the cabin-door. One day I pulled him down and whipped him while he lay prone on the ground, with

his eyes covered. I took away his food and water. He must have been downright hungry before I fed him. He never forgot the lesson. After that, when he saw me lock up he would sneak into his cage, fearful, I suppose, that if found outside he would be whipped and starved.[5]

Later, Walton shares the poignant observation that, 'night after night, in the nutting season, [the raccoon] would call to his comrades, and they would answer from the surrounding woods.' There is a jarring disconnect between the author's acknowledgement of a raccoon's ability to 'reason as well as the average human being' and his willingness to brutalize the animal to compel obedience to his human will, but this is sadly common in such accounts.[6]

Raccoons have been made into companions for as long as they have lived among humans, and they continue to be so in spite of laws against the practice in many jurisdictions. Even today many kits come into captivity as orphans, either through the inadvertent or intentional killing of their mothers, and their seeming combination of precocious pseudo-human infant and vulnerable furry baby adds to their appeal. Their intelligence means that they can be easily trained, and their wilfulness is adorable when they are small and more easily dominated. As they get older, stronger and more defiant, such qualities are less appealing. Sadly, the end result of many of these pet-making attempts is misery for the animals. We so often expect an animal to behave like a docile little human in a fur coat, and such expectations are rife with dangers for both species, although raccoons obviously get the worse of it.

Not all these encounters end badly, of course, especially when raccoons are understood as thinking beings in their own right with their own interests, customs and behaviours, and when kinship, not domination, is the foundation for shared living. The

raccoon who lived in the childhood family teepee of Santee Dakota doctor, writer and activist Charles Alexander Eastman (Ohíye S'a in Dakota) seems to have been more of a companion by mutual agreement than a controlled domesticated animal, an attitude Eastman expanded upon in 'Wechah the Provider', his 1904 short story about Wasula, a Dakota girl, and the raccoon Wechah, who together save her community from starvation during a terrible winter by hunting and trapping when the camp's hunters are killed by Ojibway raiders. Throughout the story Eastman indicates the looseness of Dakota claims over the animals. Wechah's mischief in the Dakota camp is widely tolerated, and although Wasula's people explicitly hunt raccoons for food and fur, they also recognize raccoon personhood and relationality as something distinct from but no less real than the ways of human beings.[7]

Yet this is not the common trajectory for such relationships. Raccoons were White House pets in both the Coolidge and Hoover administrations, but the most famous by far was Rebecca, a favourite pet of First Lady Grace Coolidge.[8] In 1926 Rebecca was sent to President Calvin Coolidge by a Mississippi supporter, Vinney Joyce, to be the main course of the White House Thanksgiving dinner. Coolidge was well known for his love of animals; after Theodore Roosevelt, he had the most diverse collection of live animals in residence at the White House, which included a pygmy hippo, a donkey and bears. The *Boston Herald* took pains to note that the urbane New Englander Coolidge had 'never been known to eat raccoon meat', and northern media coverage treated the story with patronizing amusement.[9] Rebecca was spared becoming a meal and soon sported an embroidered collar and a chain fixed firmly to Mrs Coolidge's arm, entertaining White House visitors and annoying staff in equal measure. While a wild raccoon companion was eventually procured for Rebecca, neither she nor the unwilling Reuben found the arrangement appealing; he soon escaped, while Rebecca was sent to the National Zoo, where she died not long after, seemingly unable to adjust to non-pet life.[10]

Although books, the Internet and popular culture abound with stories of pet raccoons and their doting human keepers, from young children to military leaders to those enjoying weekends away at their holiday cottages, most cases of attempted domestication of wildlife have a similar conclusion. Untold numbers of pet raccoons have been released back into the wild when no longer cute and controllable kits; unfamiliar with avoiding predators or feeding and foraging for themselves, unsocialized with other animals and now entirely stripped of the only social network they have known, this act is almost invariably a death sentence.

Yet survival, too, can create problems, especially in areas where raccoons are considered an invasive species and overwhelm vulnerable ecologies. And as even a cursory review of YouTube raccoon pet videos demonstrates, many of those raccoons who continue life as pets have been so over-indulged with sugary and processed foods that they can barely walk. This was certainly the case with Bandit, the world's heaviest raccoon. His human keeper insisted that he was overweight due to a 'thyroid problem', but also freely admitted to indulging his seemingly endless taste for fatty chips, blue raspberry Slushies and other junk food.[11] Overfeeding of pets is also a dominating form of behavioural control, but under the guise of affection and generosity.

Many municipalities prohibit the domestication of wildlife, both domestic and 'exotic', and there can be truly tragic consequences when pet raccoons come into contact with wildlife control and law enforcement, especially in the age of social media. In 2013 videos featuring Tennessee resident Mark 'Coonrippy' Brown with his pet raccoons, Rebekah and Gunshow, went viral. The contrast of the burly, bearded, overall-wearing Brown grooving with a seemingly entertained Gunshow on his porch to Aretha Franklin's 'Chain of Fools' resulted in more than 2 million views on YouTube, but the video had an unanticipated consequence: Tennessee wildlife officials confiscated Rebekah and, as they claimed, transported her to a rehabilitation centre for eventual release or, as Brown fretted, euthanized her (a not uncommon end for confiscated animals habituated to living with humans).[12]

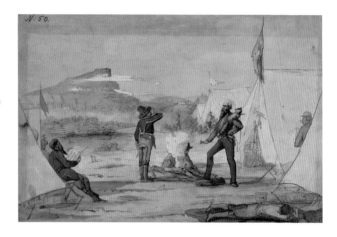

General August Willich and his pet raccoon near Lookout Mountain, Tennessee, during the U.S. Civil War. Watercolour and graphite by Adolph Metzner, c. 1861–5.

As impressively effective predators, raccoons can also be unpredictable and dangerous pets, and with their dexterity, strength, and rending claws and teeth, can do a great deal of damage, not just to property but also to flesh. Coonhounds are often mutilated by hunted raccoons, and some are permanently disabled or even killed in the scuffle. Injuries to humans can be terrible, too. One of the most widely publicized examples was in 2000, when an infant, Charlotte Ponce, was mauled by the family's pet raccoon, resulting in years of extensive facial reconstruction surgeries. In 2019 two Michigan children were attacked by a neighbour's pet raccoon, Bandit, while playing in their yard. Bandit's owners had previously released him into the wild, with the now sadly predictable result: the desperate raccoon returned to the only home and family it had known, searching for food. After the attack, one of the children received rabies shots, and Bandit was captured and killed by authorities.[13]

Like other animals relegated to the category of vermin, raccoons are frequently associated with communicable disease, especially

168

the dreaded spectre of rabies. While bats and dogs are responsible for most worldwide animal-to-human transmissions, and although rabid raccoons are far more likely to attack other animals than us, raccoon-derived rabies remains a significant public health concern, although one with necessary caveats. In their cultural history of the feared disease, Bill Wasik and Monica Murphy have identified the raccoon as 'the u.s. species most frequently found to be infected with rabies'. Yet this was not always the case:

> The spread of rabies among raccoons has been described by the [Centers for Disease Control] as 'one of the most intensive wildlife rabies outbreaks in history', and a human blunder seems to have been at least partly to blame. Before the mid-1970s, raccoon rabies . . . was confined to Florida and neighbouring states . . . But starting in 1977, more than thirty-five hundred raccoons were legally trapped in

This photograph of a yawning raccoon reveals the animal's imposing canines, only one of its adaptations for hunting and carnivory. For all their cuteness, raccoons are wild animals and evolved to be predators, as many humans inclined to making them into pets have learned to their regret.

Not among the most common vector species for animal-to-human transmission, rabies is nevertheless a real danger to raccoons and other animals, especially in North America.

ALERT

RABID RACCOONS FOUND
12/29/08 and 1/08/09
In Dumbarton Oaks Park area
AVOID ALL CONTACT WITH RACCOONS
KEEP PETS ON LEASH
If you see a raccoon showing UNUSUAL behavior or a dead carcass, please call
DC Animal Control 202-576-6664
National Park Service 202-895-6221
US Park Police at 202-426-7717.
DC Department of Health 202-535-2323

Florida and shipped to private fishing clubs in Virginia, where they were released as prospective game . . . Within three decades, rabid raccoons had been observed throughout the entire eastern United States, with a few cases sighted as far west as Ohio.[14]

As is so often the case, the animal is blamed for the consequences of human foolishness. The authors further chronicle a harrowing raccoon rabies outbreak in Manhattan, and the fear that gripped many New Yorkers who frequented that elite borough. As we have repeatedly seen, the liminal space that raccoons inhabit between domestication and wildness is a tenuous one. The mere suspicion of rabies infection is enough to turn raccoon populations from tolerated co-inhabitants to a pest targeted for widespread extermination.

Yet it does not require the threat of fatal contagion for raccoons to be considered vermin. Take this headline from a 2010 *New York Times* article: 'After Bedbugs, Here Come the Raccoons', which chronicles a growing animosity towards raccoons and their increasing conflicts with humans. As the author, Fernanda Santos, notes: 'Raccoons may be wild animals, but they're no longer a rarity in the city. They seem to be appearing in greater numbers and, like true New Yorkers, seem to be behaving much more boldly.'[15] That boldness manifests in behaviours seen by uninformed human inhabitants of the city as menacing, dangerous or simply unwelcome: the behaviours of those deemed outlaws and trespassers against the perceived social – and ostensibly natural – order. The association of raccoons with the city's even more vilified bedbugs pushes them further into the category of vermin, and this attitude extends far beyond New York.

In the early twentieth century, Ernest Thompson Seton referred to the raccoon as 'the Dryad of the hollow trees', a pre-eminent

Raccoon kit in a u.s. experimental fur farm in the Adirondack Mountains of northeastern New York State, 1919.

North American wilderness icon. For city dwellers in many countries today the animal is far more likely to be derisively labelled the 'trash panda' of the modern urban jungle and treated with the disdain afforded other successful scavengers on the fringes of human abundance.[16] Raccoons were likely among the cargo taken to Spain from the Caribbean on Christopher Columbus's first resource raid on the Americas in 1492, but it was not until the twentieth century that self-sustaining populations of raccoons were to be found outside of the Western Hemisphere. These are largely descendants of escapees from fur farms and animal parks and, as noted above, the intentional wild release of former pets.

It is important to reinforce this key point: *all* 'invasive' raccoon populations were introduced to those habitats *by humans*. The responsibility and blame therefore should be ours, but without exception these non-native populations are fiercely persecuted as morally culpable vermin. As smart and behaviourally flexible omnivores in places where they have few if any natural predators, raccoons often flourish in these new habitats, with significant impacts on local ecologies that did not evolve to accommodate the species' particular biology, habits or endemic diseases. Raccoons have also been blamed for damage to much-loved but vulnerable architecture easily destroyed by their claws, urine and faeces – mostly in Japan and Europe, but now in Russia, Iran and other countries.

The Japanese case is perhaps the strangest. The first reported raccoon naturalization in Japan was in 1962, when a group of the animals escaped a zoo in the city of Inuyama in Aichi Prefecture.[17] Intentional release by breeders and pet owners continued in the 1970s and '80s, and this is where the real trouble started.[18] As previously noted, Sterling North's popular 1963 story of his pet raccoon, *Rascal*, was adapted into an animated television series in Japan in 1977. The playful raccoon character in *Araiguma Rasukaru* beguiled Japanese child and adult viewers alike, and soon North American raccoon kits were being imported into the country or purchased from local captive populations, delighting families across the country . . . for a while. Yet as North himself learned with Rascal, cute raccoon kits are less charming when they reach sexual maturity, and as the introduced animals grew older, more rambunctious and more destructive, many Japanese families followed North's literary and animated example and released the raccoons into the wild; other raccoons escaped captivity on their own and joined the growing population.[19] Whereas the real Rascal likely succumbed to predation, exposure, starvation or disease, the raccoons of Japan found themselves and one another in a more hospitable environment, and their numbers have since exploded. Most of the country's 47 prefectures now report naturalized raccoon populations and associated problems such as damage to native ecosystems, agriculture and human property, especially 'important cultural assets such as shrines and temples'.[20]

Today raccoons are designated a major environmental menace in Japan, among the most concerning of the many exotic species introduced to the country following its post-Second World War economic recovery. Their impact is significant: expensive damage to crops, fisheries and poultry farms; widespread predation on imperilled native species including small mammals, reptiles, amphibians, birds, invertebrates, shellfish and wild plants. They disrupt habitat for local and migratory birds alike, and displace native canid competitors like the red fox and raccoon dog; they sometimes attack household pets and livestock, harass human food merchants and spread disease to other species. In urban areas they harvest home garden ponds with prized goldfish and carp and have an affinity for denning in classical wooden Shintō and Buddhist architecture.[21] Indeed, authorities estimate that up to 80 per cent of the country's temples and shrines have experienced

Commemorative stamps for the 1977 Japanese animated series *Araiguma Rasukaru*.

raccoon damage.[22] Shintō sites seem to have been considered particularly auspicious locations for wild release due to the tradition's reverence for the natural world; the resulting raccoon-wrought destruction seems an ironic and painful blow.

Japan's 2004 passage of the Invasive Species Act ostensibly provided a foundation for further interventions ranging from nuisance management to full-on extermination programmes. Authorities kill thousands of raccoons annually, but local officers tasked with raccoon issues have cited structural, training and administrative obstacles to their work, and raccoon numbers keep growing, especially as there is comparatively little public support for raccoon eradication in most prefectures in Japan even now, although that may be changing.[23]

The language used to refer to introduced raccoons in most countries is often quite troubling – it is the xenophobic terminology of alien invasion, furry trespassers who do not know their own place, a presumption of malevolent, even diabolical intent. Gesturing at the debunked rumour that the first raccoons in Germany were deliberately released into the wild by Nazi Reichsmarschall Hermann Göring as an odd premeditated act of biological warfare, the UK tabloid *The Sun* declared the population growth of introduced raccoons in that country a 'furry blitzkrieg' of 'Nazi raccoons' in 2007, directly comparing the raccoon expansion to the German invasion of France, Belgium and the Netherlands in the Second World War.[24] Both the raccoon and the raccoon dog have been identified as invasive threats by Swedish authorities, who fear the ecological impact of both species.[25] In 2013 Madrid 'declared war on invaders that threaten the peace of mind of the Spanish capital's human residents and the survival of native species of birds and animals', with conservation officials describing raccoon and Argentinian green parrot populations as having reached 'plague proportions'.[26] A 2016 *Daily Mail* headline warned 'Fears of a Raccoon Invasion as Sightings Across Britain Grow', although the story itself was rather tame compared to that of an online *Business Insider* headline that same year, which declared: 'Germany Is Overrun with Raccoons – and the Rest of the Continent Is Worried They'll Be Next', where the stereotype of uncontrolled lawlessness and destruction dominates. The story briefly notes the origins of the 'invasion' – namely, the importation of raccoons by *German* furriers and deliberate release by *German* hunting enthusiasts – but this important fact is largely buried by the rhetoric of threat, wherein raccoons become a ravenous alien horde bent on destroying German homes, habitat and species. The reporter mentions that more than 60,000 raccoons are killed annually, but with none of the condemnatory undertones; indeed the killing is presented as a necessary good for the benefit of native lives and livelihoods.[27] Whatever the intention of the writers themselves, the readily employed language of invasion, war, survival, infestation and threat is part of a larger and

Once thoroughly associated with the wilderness, today's 'trash pandas' are more likely to be considered an exclusively urban phenomenon.

troubling pattern, with ugly echoes of anti-immigrant racism and nativism in the representations of 'invasive' species.

Not all intentional or even accidental introductions have succeeded. To date Iceland has had three documented indigenous encounters with raccoons, and most ended badly: the first seven animals were brought in as pets in 1932, but most died or were killed; in 1975 three raccoons were purchased from the Copenhagen Zoo for Hafnarfjörður Aquarium, but one escaped en route and was later shot. The third incident was in 1998, when a Toronto raccoon was trapped in a pallet of hot tubs delivered to Reykjavík. Dehydrated, malnourished and disoriented from the accidental journey, it, too, was killed by police.[28]

In spite of wildlife officials' best efforts to stop them, raccoons have been sighted in most European countries, although some of these sightings are of individuals only – likely abandoned or escaped pets – and not evidence of breeding populations. Yet authorities are increasingly concerned about the latter, as in Spain, where raccoon expansion in Madrid and its surrounding biodiversity region threatens native plants and animals as well as migratory birds.[29] Russia has had a domestic raccoon population since 1936, introduced and released for its fur and quickly establishing itself throughout the territories of the then-Soviet Union. In 1996 their numbers exceeded 40,000, although the inhospitably cold climate and hunting have kept the population smaller than in other countries with milder weather and lower predation pressures.[30] Raccoons were released in Poland in 1945 for hunting sport and fur trapping, and their range has expanded significantly since then. Raccoons also have an increasing population presence in the Gilan Province of northern Iran.[31]

For those hoping to limit or entirely eliminate raccoons from their local environments, the news is not good. Not only are raccoons exceptionally adaptive to a diverse range of habitats and

An inquiring raccoon peeks through leaves in Costa Rica.

food sources, a rapidly changing climate has made many more regions suitable for dramatic raccoon expansion. In 2016 a group of scientists used complex computer modelling to assess current data and predict future raccoon range. With increasingly favourable precipitation and temperature levels across areas of the world that had once been inhospitable to the species, the scientists predicted that '61% of the world is considered to be suitable for the raccoon invasion'.[32]

From catastrophic population decline to global expansion and major ecological disruption in less than a century: this is a rare species success story, one with more than a few similarities to our own. In spite of all the ways we have misunderstood, misrepresented and mistreated them, raccoons have endured; if anything, they are stronger now than ever. So we finish this book by considering raccoon futures. Although it is perhaps too early to posit a looming Procyocene epoch, one thing is certainly clear: raccoons are on the rise, and we would do well to pay attention.

Epilogue: Arakun Triumphant?

When eagles and buffalo have long disappeared, when all America has become one vast expressway and used-car lot, the raccoon will still be with us – nesting in rusty automobile bodies, eating cast-off TV dinners, drinking water that collects in old tires.
Polly Redford, 'Our Most American Animal'[1]

What might a world look like if raccoons, not humans, were the dominant species? Our simian success story is, in many ways, an accident of evolution, the good fortune of a particularly flexible and creative omnivore with a capacity for sociality and inclinations to violent territoriality. While commentators frequently joke about too-smart raccoons becoming our future animal overlords, there are enough similarities between our species to make such scenarios uncomfortable to consider.

The science fiction writer Steven R. Boyett made this narrative conceit the foundation of his cult classic novel *The Architect of Sleep* (1986). The book's protagonist, James Bentley, stumbles into an alternate North America when a solitary spelunking expedition in Florida goes awry after he passes through a strange shimmering curtain in a previously unexplored part of the cave network. Upon emerging, he finds himself in another world, one with the same native flora and fauna but in abundance far beyond that of his own ecologically ravaged 1980s Florida. Here the Florida panther is no longer critically endangered, manatees and cranes travel in abundance and without fear, invasive water hyacinths are absent, and bipedal, llama-riding raccoons live, love, and wage war in their world of two moons.

Bentley is soon captured by one of the raccoon folk, a rock-slinging, battle-scarred and formidable female seer of her kind, and

This dapper, bespectacled raccoon by Russian artist BrainEater/ Vadim Poleshchuck hints at an otherwise reality with *Procyon lotor*, not *Homo sapiens*, as the dominant global species.

from here the story closely hews to the classic captivity narrative structure wherein a frightened and naive interloper gradually learns about the culture and moral condition of their native captors. As Bentley learns, so too does the reader. And there is much to learn. He names his host Truck after a pet raccoon from his college days, but she is no pet: she is a True Dreamer who had been waiting for his arrival, for she has seen that he is destined to help her regain her rightful position as Architect of Sleep, a position she lost to a tyrannical usurper. But all of this is only gradually revealed, for although she does make vocalizations, it is not verbal speech that bridges their understanding: her people's primary way of communicating is through a complex sign language, a nod to the raccoon's dextrous and sensitive forepaws. Just as Bentley is at first baffled by Truck's seeming lack of complex speech, she, too, finds his communication style frustrating: 'He is odd, to be walking so thin and high on two long legs. And the noises from him! Unceasingly, the noises. Like the birds in the trees, but deeper.'[2]

Much of the early part of the novel is their struggle to understand one another. Bentley realizes that raccoon speech is far different from the American Sign Language with which he has some slight familiarity, largely because it is based on raccoon cognition, not that of *Homo sapiens*:

It's really a very frustrating thing that a language based on hand signing is of necessity conceptually different from one that is spoken. Truck and I – and every über-raccoon I shall introduce in this account – were completely incapable of expressing each other's names in the other's 'tongue'. Truck's name is a hand motion, as is that of every other raccoon. Consequently I am unable to write it down – for though the name has a graphic analogue in their written

language, it, too, would mean nothing if I wrote it down; it would just look like streamlined Chinese.[3]

Bentley gradually learns to interpret her signs but in doing so also reflects more deeply on his own culture, and as their understanding deepens and the full import of his presence in this world is revealed, Boyett's world grows more complex and compelling. The novel is as much a study of multispecies understanding as it is the story of a looming war between Truck's faithful followers and the treacherous Stripes – the equivalent of a raccoon soldiery – who have assisted in her ousting. There is much that is familiar in this novel – fear, curiosity, love, conflict – but much that hints at diverse ways of being, richly textured sensory and conceptual worlds that have their roots in the other-than-human beings with whom we already share our existence.

As Boyett's readers have noted in various online forums, the novel is also phenomenally frustrating, for in spite of all the imaginative world-building it ends *in medias res* because of a conflict between the author and his publisher, and the planned five-book series was cut short after just the single volume. Boyett has repeatedly declined to finish the story, even after regaining the publication rights.

Yet in some ways the epic's abrupt truncation seems somehow appropriate, especially in the discussion here. For we are part of an extraordinarily varied and complex world of our own, on the edge of a future that is similarly unknowable, and absent the predictive visions of a True Dreamer, there is much to both hope for and fear. Boyett's thus-far-unfinished speculative story about

Raccoon at the Artis Royal Zoo in Amsterdam.

bipedal raccoons as our planet's dominant species presents a world not entirely unfamiliar from our own, and something resembling the evolutionary trajectory he imagines is one that may well be underway.

If that is the case, it is likely not going to happen in Florida, but 2,000 km (1,250 mi.) to the north, in Toronto, Ontario.

Designer Rob Collinet's 'Toronto Trash Pandas' reimagining of the Toronto Blue Jays baseball team logo, 2013.

While the status is thus far unofficial in the Canadian city itself, even the U.S.'s National Public Radio has declared Toronto to be the raccoon capital of the world. There is a flourishing souvenir industry of raccoon-themed Toronto kitsch available online or in merchandise stores, with knee-high socks, T-shirts, patches and other raccoonish paraphernalia emphasizing the association between raccoons and Canada's largest urban centre. A raccoon was one of only two graphic icons on the city's 'TO Canada with Love' street signs celebrating Canada's 150th anniversary (the other being a Canadian maple leaf). In 2015 sportswear company Nike participated with a localized campaign in the city's popular Queen Street West neighbourhood, placing a huge inflatable raccoon atop a building with the Nike 'swoosh' in its mouth, clearly torn from the billboard beneath it. The billboard text read 'When your city's raccoons are as big as dogs, you don't jog. You run.'[4] A dead raccoon on a hot summer section of city pavement in 2015 led to an outpouring of mingled anger and sympathy in person and online, and the site became a makeshift protest site/funeral tribute to 'Conrad', complete with a rose, a candle and a framed raccoon photo. Even a brief perusal of the city newspapers gives a sense of Torontonians' fascination with raccoon-related news items: 'Mayor Declares War on Raccoons' (2015), 'Raccoon Causes Subway Delay in Toronto' (2016), 'Toronto Woman Wakes Up to Raccoon Sex' (2016), 'Raccoon Family Takes

In July 2015, when Toronto city staff took twelve hours to collect the body of a dead raccoon from a sidewalk in the city's sweltering downtown, residents began to amass a tongue-in-cheek shrine to 'Conrad' in quiet protest and sympathy.

Over Toronto Bank' (2017), 'Raccoons Bust into Toronto Woman's Home, Stare Her Down While Defiantly Eating Her Bread' (2017), 'Toronto Raccoon Rescued after Head Gets Stuck in Jar' (2018) and the perennial question, 'Is Toronto the Raccoon Capital of Canada?' (2019). (Journalist Jim Rankin went even further back in Toronto's newspaper archives to find two full envelopes of raccoon-related news stories dating at least to the 1930s, noting that few 'subjects in the pre-digital age merited one envelope, let alone two'.[5]) While some Torontonians despise this four-legged city dweller, there is no doubt that many residents and tourists alike are fascinated by this increasingly visible (and lucrative) icon of the city. It is certainly no less objectionable than many of its legitimately elected human representatives past and present.

There are many reasons for raccoon prominence in Toronto, but one of the most important is sheer numbers: Toronto is estimated to be home to fifty times more raccoons than in surrounding areas, and that increased density, along with abundant food supplies in the way of human garbage, a relatively predator-free habitat (aside from occasional coyotes, domestic dogs and automobile traffic), and a complex, ever-changing environment that selects for more intellectually flexible individuals for longer-term survival, all contribute to a raccoon population that is ever more engaged with its human neighbours. (Chicago is Toronto's main competition in the 'official raccoon city' rankings, but its residents seem not to share the same vocal and commercial interest in the species.) In the 2011 documentary *Raccoon Nation*, film-makers posited that, because of these habitat qualities, Toronto's raccoons are developing at a faster pace than in other areas, what researcher and contributor Suzanne MacDonald has elsewhere wryly deemed 'an evolutionary arms race' wherein humans are witnessing the emergence of the larger, smarter 'über raccoon' and struggling to keep up.[6]

Yet while raccoons in Toronto seem to be thriving, the news is not all good: as human refuse is a major food source for these urban raccoons, scientists are also witnessing a significant rise in illnesses associated with our own processed and sugar-rich diets, including increased rates of tooth decay, weight gain and reduction in body condition, and negative impacts on glucose metabolism.[7] As they become increasingly dependent on human rubbish for food, any substantial change to diet and waste management practices may have profound negative consequences on the animals. Increased density also means more risk for contagious disease, especially distemper, which can quickly burn through a city's raccoon population.

Right now, however, raccoons in most areas are doing well enough for many to wonder: what next? And how do we respond? Evolutionarily advanced über-raccoons seem entirely the stuff of science fiction, but the changes are well within the realm of reality; add to this the almost fantastical scenario of irradiated raccoons now expanding alongside rising wild boar numbers in the Fukushima Daiichi Nuclear Power Plant evacuation zone,

A mother raccoon teaches her attentive kits how to harvest and eat maize in this 1937 painting.

Artist James Ng describes his delightfully quirky *Raccoon Express* (2013) thusly: 'A combination of steam ingenuity and street food culture, the Raccoon Express is a famous attraction of the Imperial City. A catchy tune performed by the chimney-bots signals its arrival and entices the public. A pack of trained raccoons trail the Express, cleaning up any mess left behind by the hungry mob near the tracks.'

animals that cannot easily be managed because of contamination risks. Between the disruptions of anthropogenic climate change, evolutionary adaptation due to human-induced habitat and food changes, and now something akin to atomic raccoons, what seemed to once be entirely in the realm of raccoon fantasy now feels not that far from plausible.

In Boyett's novel, Truck, the True Dreamer of the raccoon-people, looks to the future with both fear and anticipation. Her world is being transformed by the prophesied Bald Ape, James Bentley, and his actions will determine not only her survival but the well-being of her society, perhaps even her very world. This, too, has the ring of familiarity. That fictional future remains unpublished, just as ours is unwritten, but both offer peril and possibility for those who continue.

The future for raccoons is, in many ways, the future for all of the creation, and humanity's actions will in large part determine both. Just as our ancestors co-evolved in this world with theirs, and just as we have lived alongside one another for thousands of years, so too will we all share what is yet to come. But the moral burden of that responsibility is ours, not theirs, for they have merely adapted to the world we have transformed and, in many cases, deformed, as the writer and urban geographer Amy Lavender Harris reflects:

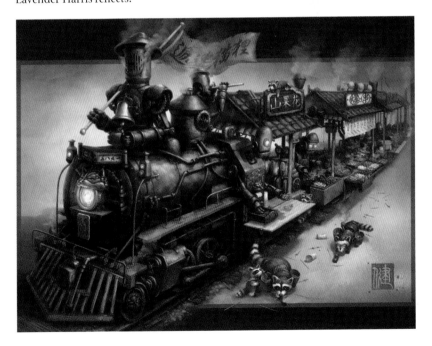

Perhaps . . . we should think of the spread-out contents of our Green Bins as offerings, a sort of tithing we do to make up for some of the destruction we have wrought upon the natural world. In this sense – because they know the secrets of our excess – we should think of raccoons as confessors, or at the very least, as Sin-Eaters, who absorb our transgressions and, therefore, help redeem us.[8]

Whether raccoons should be expected to bear that redemptive burden or not, there is certainly much we can learn from them about how to survive, even thrive, in a swiftly changing world, and there is much we can do to make their own struggles less difficult. That possibility, however, depends entirely on whether we continue to regard them as unwanted vermin and despised outlaws, or if we instead approach them with humility and generosity as other-than-human kin with as much right to flourish in this world as we have.

Given just how successfully they have managed to deal with the impact of our negative attitudes thus far, the latter may be the wiser option, for all our sakes.

A raccoon takes
an evening ramble
across a log in
Stanley Park,
Vancouver,
Canada.

Timeline of the Raccoon

20 MYA

First true procyonids evolve in North and Central America

2.5 MYA

Great American Biotic Interchange enables procyonids to expand to South America

900 CE–c. 1730

Raccoons and related imagery figure prominently in Mississippian art from across the American Southeast

1834

White minstrel singer-songwriter George Washington Dixon popularizes the stereotyped figure of Zip Coon in the racist vernacular

1840

Whig William Henry Harrison adopts the raccoon as his symbol in his 'log cabin and hard cider' campaign for the U.S. presidency

1963

Sterling North's *Rascal: A Memoir of a Better Era* is published

1971

Joint Resolution 156 of the 87th General Assembly declares the raccoon the official state wild animal of Tennessee

1976

Bill Mantlo's Rocket Raccoon first appears in *Marvel Preview 7* and receives his own miniseries nine years later

1977

The animated adaptation of North's *Rascal* airs in Japan, spurring enthusiasm for pet raccoons and marking the onset of the raccoon invasion of the country

1492	1608	1740	1831
Christopher Columbus encounters the 'clownlike dog' – likely a raccoon – on his first pillaging raid in the Americas	The Powhatan word *arakun* enters English as 'Rahaughcum' in John Smith's *A True Relation*	Linnaeus identifies raccoons as long-tailed bears, then as washer bears in 1758; Storr places them in their own *Procyon* genus in 1780	James Kirke Paulding's *The Lion of the West* coonskin-wearing spoof of Davy Crockett is so popular that the real Crockett adopts the fashion while campaigning for Congress

1926	1928	1930s	1954
Rebecca the raccoon is spared becoming the Coolidge family's Thanksgiving dinner and instead takes up residence in the White House	The Klages and Coots song 'Doin' the Raccoon' captures the spirit of the raccoon coat craze in vogue on college and university campuses across the U.S.	Raccoon populations reach their nadir in North America	Fess Parker appears as Davy Crockett on Walt Disney's debut *Disneyland* show, launching a coonskin cap phenomenon

1995	2014		2016
The world is introduced to Meeko, the mischievous raccoon companion of Disney's eponymous Pocahontas	Rocket Raccoon, voiced by actor Bradley Cooper, debuts on the big screen in the Marvel film *Guardians of the Galaxy*		A group of scientists predict that 61 per cent of the Earth is now suitable habitat for raccoon population expansion

References

INTRODUCTION: AN UNCANNY OUTLAW

1 Charles G. D. Roberts, *The Watchers of the Trails: A Book of Animal Life* (London, 1904), p. 212.

2 Personal interview with Suzanne MacDonald, Vancouver, British Columbia, 13 September 2019.

3 Kiri Blakely, 'Art-loving Criminals: Four Raccoons Caught "Burglarizing" Gallery Go Viral after Cops Post Their Hilariously Incriminating Photo', *Daily Mail* (14 November 2015), www.dailymail.co.uk.

4 Samuel I. Zeveloff, *Raccoons: A Natural History* (Washington, DC, and London, 2002), pp. 160–61.

1 THE BEAST ITSELF: RACCOON NATURAL HISTORY

1 Vance Joseph Hoyt, *Bar-Rac: The Biography of a Raccoon* (Boston, MA, 1931), p. 18.

2 Samuel I. Zeveloff offers a fascinating history of the raccoon's changing taxonomy in *Raccoons: A Natural History* (Washington, DC, and London, 2002), pp. 3–7.

3 Virginia C. Holmgren, *Raccoons in History, Folklore and Today's Backyards* (Santa Barbara, CA, 1990), pp. 159, 49.

4 Zeveloff, *Raccoons: A Natural History*, p. 6.

5 Klaus-Peter Koepfli et al., 'Phylogeny of the Procyonidae (Mammalia: Carnivora): Molecules, Morphology and the Great American Interchange', *Molecular Phylogenetics and Evolution*, XVIII (2007), p. 1086.

6 Ibid., pp. 1086–7.

7 Monique Grooten and Rosamunde Almond, eds, wwf *Living Planet Report – 2018: Aiming Higher* (Gland, Switzerland, 2018), p. 7.

8 R. Timm et al., '*Procyon lotor*', *The iucn Red List of Threatened Species*, www.iucnredlist.org, 2016.

9 Woop Studios, *A Compendium of Collective Nouns: From an Armory of Aardvarks to a Zeal of Zebras* (San Francisco, ca, 2013), p. 166.

10 Captain Mayne Reid, *The Hunter's Feast; or, Conversations around the Camp-fire* (London, 1855), p. 93.

11 François-Marc Gagnon, with Nancy Senior and Réal Ouellet, *The Codex Canadensis and the Writings of Louis Nicolas* (Tulsa, ok, Montreal, and Kingston, Ontario, 2011), pp. 158–9, 315–16. Zeveloff offers further commentary on the Erie-wildcat–raccoon confusion, in *Raccoons: A Natural History*, pp. 168–9.

12 Zeveloff, *Raccoons: A Natural History*, p. 167.

13 Mark Catesby, *The Natural History of Carolina, Florida and the Bahama Islands*, vol. i (London, 1731), p. xxix.

14 Luke Hunter, *Carnivores of the World* (Princeton, nj, 2011), p. 134.

15 David Slade, 'Rotund Raccoon's Record Life Ends', *Chicago Tribune*, www.chicagotribune.com, 13 May 2004.

16 See Zeveloff, *Raccoons: A Natural History*, pp. 94–5.

17 Marc Zender, 'The Raccoon Glyph in Classic Maya Writing', pari *Journal* (2005), pp. 7–8.

18 Ernest Thompson Seton, *Life-histories of Northern Animals*, vol. ii (New York, 1909), p. 1017.

19 Personal interview with Suzanne MacDonald, Vancouver, British Columbia, 13 September 2019.

20 P. W. Bateman and P. A. Fleming, 'Big City Life: Carnivores in Urban Environments', *Journal of Zoology*, cclxxxvii (2012), p. 14.

21 Ray Allen Billington and Martin Ridge, *Westward Expansion: A History of the American Frontier*, 6th edn (Albuquerque, nm, 2011), p. 103.

22 Seton, *Life-histories of Northern Animals*, p. 1017.

23 'Is Toronto the Raccoon Capital of Canada?', *The National*, Canadian Broadcasting Corporation, 16 July 2019.

24 Michael Pettit, 'The Problem of Raccoon Intelligence in Behaviourist America', *British Journal for the History of Science*, XLIII/3 (September 2010), p. 402.

25 Ibid., p. 394.

26 Ernest Ingersoll, *Wild Neighbors: Out-door Studies in the United States* (London, 1906), pp. 275–6.

27 Ibid., p. 280.

28 Lauren Stanton et al., 'Adaptation of the Aesop's Fable Paradigm for Use with Raccoons (*Procyon lotor*)', *Animal Cognition*, XX (2017), pp. 1148–9.

29 Holmgren, *Raccoons in History*, pp. 157–61.

30 Bradley M. Arsznov and Sharleen T. Sakai, 'The Procyonid Social Club', *Brain, Behavior and Evolution*, LXXXII/2 (October 2013), pp. 129–31.

31 C. Newman, C. D. Buesching and J. O. Wolff, 'The Function of Masks in "Midguild" Carnivores', *Oikos*, CVIII/3 (March 2005), p. 633.

2 RACCOONS OF SYMBOL AND STORY

1 William J. Long, *A Little Brother to the Bear and Other Animal Studies* (Toronto, 1903), p. 20.

2 See James Mooney, *History, Myths, and Sacred Formulas of the Cherokees* (Asheville, NC, 1992), pp. 286–7.

3 Susan C. Power, *Early Art of the Southeastern Indians: Feathered Serpents and Winged Beings* (Athens, GA, 2004), p. 183.

4 Ibid., pp. 183–4.

5 John Smith, *A Map of Virginia* (Oxford, 1612), p. 13.

6 Frank G. Speck, *Ceremonial Songs of the Creek and Yuchi Indians* (Philadelphia, PA, 1911), p. 233.

7 William A. Read, *Louisiana Place Names of Indian Origin: A Collection of Words* (Tuscaloosa, AL, 2008), p. 102.

8 Virginia C. Holmgren, *Raccoons: In History, Folklore and Today's Backyards* (Santa Barbara, CA, 1990), pp. 157–61.

9 Christopher B. Teuton et al., *Cherokee Stories of the Turtle Island Liars' Club* (Chapel Hill, NC, 2012), p. 197.

10 Daphne Odjig, *Nanabush Punishes the Raccoon* (Boston, 1971); John Borrows, *Recovering Canada: The Resurgence of Indigenous Law* (Toronto, 2002), p. 205.

11 Liz Kickham and Leroy Sealy, 'Teaching Stories: Cultural and Educational Uses of Traditional and Personal Narrative in the Choctaw Language Classroom', *Proceedings of the Sixteenth Annual Symposium about Language and Society*, Texas Linguistic Forum, LII (2008), p. 86.

12 Brian Swann, ed., *Algonquian Spirit: Contemporary Translations of the Algonquian Literatures of North America* (Lincoln, NE, 2005), pp. 72–5, 81–3.

13 Barbara Jacobs Mitnick, 'Jean Leon Gerome Ferris: America's Painter Historian', unpublished PhD thesis, Rutgers University, 1983, pp. 328–9.

14 Ernest Thompson Seton, *Wild Animal Ways* (Garden City, NY, 1922), p. 89.

15 Clara Dillingham Pierson, *Among the Night People* (New York, 1902), p. x.

16 Terry Caesar, *Speaking of Animals: Essays on Dogs and Others* (Leiden, 2009), p. 212.

17 Stanley Kunitz, 'Raccoon Journal', in *The Collected Poems* (New York, 2000). Copyright © 1985, 1995, 2000 by Stanley Kunitz, used by permission of W. W. Norton & Company, Inc.

18 Margarita Meklina, 'Randy Raccoons: The Threat to Russia's Youth', *Brooklyn Rail* (September 2014), https://brooklynrail.org.

19 Reprinted from Gerry LaFemina, 'The Raccoon', in *New Poems from the Third Coast: Contemporary Michigan Poetry*, ed. Michael Delp, Conrad Hilberry and Josie Kearns (Detroit, MI, 2000), pp. 141–2. Copyright © 2000 Wayne State University Press, with the permission of Wayne State University Press.

3 THE RACIST COON

1 Lucille Clifton, 'What Spells Raccoon to Me', *Daedalus*, CXXXIX/3 (Summer 2010), p. 144. Copyright © 1987 by Lucille Clifton.

Reprinted with the permission of The Permissions Company, LLC on behalf of BOA Editions, Ltd., boaeditions.org.

2 Chauncey DeVega, 'The Big "Black Racism" Lie: The Toxic Right-wing Trope that Shrouds the Truth about White Supremacy', *Salon.com*, 9 October 2015.

3 Luke Fater, 'Why President Coolidge Never Ate His Thanksgiving Raccoon', *Atlas Obscura*, 26 November 2019, www.atlasobscura.com.

4 'coon, n.', *Oxford English Dictionary Online*, www.oed.com.

5 Geoffrey Hughes, *An Encyclopedia of Swearing* (London, 2006), p. 99.

6 Gerald Bordman and Richard Norton, *American Musical Theatre: A Chronicle*, 4th edn (New York, 2010), pp. 2–3; Ralph P. Locke, 'Musicology and/as Social Concern: Imagining the Relevant Musicologist', in *Rethinking Music*, ed. Nicholas Cook and Mark Everist (Oxford, 2010), p. 517.

7 Psyche A. Williams-Forson, *Building Houses Out of Chicken Legs: Black Women, Food, and Power* (Chapel Hill, NC, 2006), p. 50.

8 Barbara Lewis, 'Daddy Blue: The Evolution of the Dark Dandy', in *Inside the Minstrel Mask: Readings in Nineteenth Century Black Minstrelsy*, ed. Annemarie Bean, James Hatch and Brooks McNamara (Hanover, NH, 1996), p. 259.

9 Roland Leander Williams, Jr, *Black Male Frames: African Americans in a Century of Hollywood Cinema, 1903–2003* (Syracuse, NY, 2014), p. 19.

10 Thomas Birch, *Zip Coon: A Famous Comic Song* (New York, 1834). Dale Cockrell's *Demons of Disorder: Early Blackface Minstrels and their World* (Cambridge and New York, 1997), offers extensive context for the minstrel productions of this period.

11 David R. Roediger, *The Wages of Whiteness: Race and the Making of the American Working Class* (London and New York, 1999), p. 98.

12 James H. Dormon, 'Shaping the Popular Image of Post-Reconstruction American Blacks: The "Coon Song" Phenomenon of the Gilded Age', *American Quarterly*, XL/4 (December 1988), p. 452.

13 Nicholas W. Proctor, *Bathed in Blood: Hunting and Mastery in the Old South* (Charlottesville, VA, 2002), p. 131.

14 Captain [Thomas] Mayne Reid, *The Hunters' Feast; or, Conversations around the Camp-fire* (London, 1855), pp. 95–6.

15 William R. Black, 'How Watermelons Became a Racist Trope', *The Atlantic* (8 December 2014), available at www.theatlantic.com.

16 Edwin C. Bridges, *Alabama: The Making of an American State* (Tuscaloosa, AL, 2016), p. 159; Writer David Emery provided an extensive fact-checked history of the rooster's white supremacist uses in 'Did a State Democratic Party Logo Once Feature the Slogan "White Supremacy"?', www.snopes.com, 25 September 2017.

17 Robert J. Kloss, 'Psychodynamic Speculations on Derogatory Names for Blacks', *Journal of Black Psychology*, V/2 (February 1979), p. 89.

18 The composition of this scene is strikingly similar to that of Tenniel's illustration of Alice's first encounter with the Cheshire Cat three years later, with Alice standing in John Bull's position and the Cheshire Cat crouching in that of the Lincoln raccoon.

19 Maurice B. Wheeler, 'Politics and Race in American Historical Popular Music: Contextualized Access and Minstrel Music Archives', *Arch Sci*, XI (2011), pp. 54–5.

20 Patricia R. Schroeder, 'Passing for Black: Coon Songs and the Performance of Race', *Journal of American Culture*, XXXIII/2 (June 2010), p. 152.

21 Ibid., p. 141.

22 Williams-Forson, *Building Houses Out of Chicken Legs*, p. 56.

23 E. W. Kemble, *Comical Coons* (New York, 1898), p. 16.

24 Catherine Roth, 'The Coon Chicken Inn: North Seattle's Beacon of Bigotry', The Seattle Civil Rights and Labor History Project, 2009, https://depts.washington.edu, accessed 20 February 2020.

25 George Heinold, *Burglar in the Treetops* (New York, 1952), p. 6.

26 'Free "Coon" Hunter in St Augustine Fracas', *Pittsburgh Courier*, 27 June 1963, available online at Civil Rights Library of St Augustine, http://cdm16000.contentdm.oclc.org, accessed 14 September 2019.

27 Thérèse Smith, 'Lyrical Protest: Music in the History of African American Culture', *Human Bondage in the Cultural Contact Zone: Transdisciplinary Perspectives on Slavery and Its Discourses*, ed. Raphael Hörmann and Gesa Mackenthun (Münster, 2010), p. 264.

28 Rocky Sexton, 'Coonasses', in *The New Encyclopedia of Southern Culture*, vol. VI: *Ethnicity*, ed. Celeste Ray (Chapel Hill, NC, 2007), pp. 132–3.

29 T. J. Tallie, 'On Zulu King Cetshwayo kaMpande's Visit to London, August 1882', in *BRANCH: Britain, Representation and Nineteenth-century History*, ed. Dino Franco Felluga: Extension of *Romanticism and Victorianism on the Net*, published February 2015, www.branchcollective.org, accessed 1 March 2020.

30 Jane Battersby, 'Coon Carnival', in *Encyclopedia of Race and Racism*, ed. Patrick L. Mason, 2nd edn (Detroit, MI, 2013), p. 437.

31 Lisa Baxter, 'Continuity and Change in Cape Town's Coon Carnival: The 1960s and 1970s', *African Studies*, LX/1 (2001), pp. 87–105.

4 COONSKINS AND COON HUNTS: THE DEAD RACCOON

1 A. R. Ammons, 'Coon Song', in *The Complete Poems of A. R. Ammons*, vol. I: 1955–77, ed. Robert M. West (New York, 2017). Copyright © 1960 by A. R. Ammons, used by permission of W. W. Norton & Company Inc.

2 Bob Moore, 'Corps of Discovery Hats', *We Proceed On*, XXVII/2 (May 2001), pp. 21, 24.

3 Mitchell D. Strauss, 'Coonskin Cap', in *Ethnic Dress in the United States: A Cultural Encyclopedia*, ed. Amanda Lynch and Michael D. Strauss (Lanham, MD, 2015), p. 94.

4 Mandy Merck, 'Davy Crockett', *History Workshop Journal*, XL (Autumn 1995), pp. 187–8.

5 Samuel I. Zeveloff, *Raccoons: A Natural History* (Washington, DC, and London, 2002), p. 160.

6   Jennifer Le Zotte, *From Goodwill to Grunge: A History of Secondhand Styles and Alternative Economies* (Chapel Hill, NC, 2017), p. 128.

7   'Next Academic Year Will See $100 Increase in Tuition Fee', *Harvard Crimson* (28 February 1928), available at www.thecrimson. com.

8   Zeveloff, *Raccoons: A Natural History*, p. 160.

9   'Those Raccoon Coats', *Variety*, CIV/12 (1 December 1931), p. 46.

10 Raymond Klages and J. Fred Coots, *Doin' the Raccoon* (New York, 1928), pp. 7–8.

11 Le Zotte, *From Goodwill to Grunge*, p. 128.

12 John James Audubon, 'A Racoon Hunt in Kentucky', *Spirit of the Times*, XI/37 (13 November 1841), p. 434.

13 Wiley Prewitt, 'Coon Hounds', in *The New Encyclopedia of Southern Culture*, vol. XIV: *Folklife* (Chapel Hill, NC, 2010), p. 273.

14 Nicholas W. Proctor, *Bathed in Blood: Hunting and Mastery in the Old South* (Charlottesville, VA, 2002), p. 131.

15 Quoted in Priscilla Wakefield, *Excursions in North America, Described in Letters from a Gentleman and His Young Companion* (London, 1806), p. 83.

16 Mark Twain, *A Tramp Abroad* (New York, 1907), vol. II, pp. 239–40.

17 John Spurgeon, 'Gillett Coon Supper', *Encyclopedia of Arkansas* (posted 7 June 2018), www.encyclopediaofarkansas.net.

18 'Dr John's Raccoon Stew', WWOZ 90.7 FM website (22 June 2017), www.wwoz.org.

19 Andrew Beahrs, *Twain's Feast: Searching for America's Lost Foods in the Footsteps of Samuel Clemens* (New York, 2010), p. 66. The book's entire second chapter is largely dedicated to the eating of raccoons and possums, and is a fascinating if often unappetizing discussion.

20 Wilson Rawls, *Where the Red Fern Grows* [1961] (New York, 2016), p. 161.

21 Ibid., p. 168.

22 Jerry Clower, 'A Coon Huntin' Story', MCA, 1971.

23 Prewitt, 'Coon Hounds', p. 273.

24 'Black and Tan Coonhound', *American Kennel Club*, www.akc.org, accessed 27 August 2019.

25 Warren H. Miller, *The American Hunting Dog: Modern Strains of Bird Dogs and Hounds, and their Field Training* (New York, 1919), p. 55.

5 RASCALS AND ROCKETS: RACCOONS IN POPULAR CULTURE

1 Gregory Blake Smith, 'Hands', in *The Law of Miracles: And Other Stories* (Amherst, MA, 2011), p. 72.

2 Marcella Bush Treviño, 'Davy Crockett', *St James Encyclopedia of Popular Culture*, 2nd edn (Detroit, MI, 2013), p. 54.

3 Walt Disney, 'The Disneyland Story', *Disneyland*, American Broadcasting Company, 27 October 1954.

4 Lisa Anne Fischman, 'Coonskin Fever: Frontier Adventures in Postwar American Culture', unpublished PhD thesis, University of Minnesota, 1996, pp. 106, 117.

5 The Mattaponi and Pamunkey peoples are two of the member nations of the Powhatan Confederacy. This oral tradition is most extensively chronicled in Linwood Custalow and Angela L. Daniel, *The True Story of Pocahontas: The Other Side of History* (Golden, CO, 2007). Contemporary scholarship supports much of this interpretation.

6 *Meeko* is not a Powhatan word. The name is likely derived from Meeko (or Mikew), the mischief-making trickster Squirrel of the Algonquian-speaking Abenakian peoples (distant linguistic kin to Powhatan), or *miko*, which comes from the culturally and geographically discrete southeastern Muskogean language family and means 'chief' or 'leader'.

7 Bradford Evans, 'The Lost Roles of John Candy', *Vulture* (2 June 2011), available at www.vulture.com. The article includes a link to an early pencil test of Redfeather and his repartee with the snobbish English pug, Percy. In *Mouse under Glass: Secrets of Disney Animation and Theme Parks* (Irvine, CA, 2015), David Koenig states that Candy was only under consideration for the role when he died (p. 241).

8 'Creating Meeko', interview with Nik Ranieri, DVD bonus
   feature, *Pocahontas: 10th Anniversary Edition* (Walt Disney Home
   Entertainment, 2005).

9 See, as one example, Ross Douthat's editorial 'Heaven and Nature',
   which bemoans the reductively painted pantheism – via Disney's
   Pocahontas and *The Lion King*, *Dances with Wolves*, the Force of the
   Star Wars franchise, and, especially, James Cameron's blockbuster
   Avatar – that he claims 'has been Hollywood's religion of choice
   for a generation now' (*New York Times* online, 20 December 2009,
   www.nytimes.com).

10 Bradley Cooper, interview with Ellen DeGeneres, *The Ellen Show*,
   5 May 2017, www.ellentube.com.

11 Sharon Packer offers a provocative analysis of the comic series'
   representation of mental illness and its distinctions from the filmic
   Rocket in 'Halfworld's Loonies in *Rocket Raccoon* Comics – Serious
   or Satire?', in *Mental Illness in Popular Culture*, ed. Sharon Packer
   (Santa Barbara, CA, 2017), pp. 267–8.

12 *Guardians of the Galaxy*, written and directed by James Gunn
   (Marvel Studios, 2014).

13 Rob Keyes, 'Rocket Raccoon Is the "Heart" of *Guardians
   of the Galaxy*', *Screenrant* (18 April 2013), available at
   https://screenrant.com.

14 National Wildlife Federation, 'About Ranger Rick' (12 August
   2019), www.nwf.org.

15 Eben Lehman, 'Forgotten Characters from Forest History:
   Howdy Raccoon', *Peeling Back the Bark*, Forest History Society
   (3 December 2012), http://fhsarchives.wordpress.com.

16 'Introducing Mr Porter', Porter Airlines (31 July 2006),
   www.flyporter.com.

6 TRASH PANDA: PET AND PEST

1 John Tillotson, *Tales about Animals: by John Tillotson; Illustrated
   with Upwards of One Hundred Steel Engravings, by Lanseere, le Keux,
   Sands, and Others* (London, 1865), p. 154.

2 Lucinda Cole, *Imperfect Creatures: Vermin, Literature, and the Sciences of Life, 1600–1740* (Minneapolis, MN, 2016), pp. 1–2.

3 Yi-Fu Tuan, *Dominance and Affection: The Making of Pets* (New Haven, CT, 1984), p. 88.

4 Leon F. Whitney and Acil B. Underwood, *The Raccoon* (Orange, CT, 1952), p. 133.

5 Mason A. Walton, *A Hermit's Wild Friends, or Eighteen Years in the Woods* (Boston, MA, 1903), pp. 32–3.

6 Ibid., p. 34.

7 Charles Alexander Eastman, *Indian Boyhood* (New York, 1902), pp. 200–201; 'Wechah the Provider', *Red Hunters and the Animal People* (New York, 2004), p. 77.

8 Matthew Costello, 'Raccoons at the White House', www.whitehousehistory.org, 8 June 2018.

9 Quoted in Kate Knibbs, 'The Raccoon Who Moved into the White House on Thanksgiving' (22 November 2017), www.theringer.com.

10 Matthew L. Miller, 'A Presidential Pardon for a Thanksgiving Raccoon', www.blog.nature.com, 5 November 2018.

11 Associated Press, 'World's Heaviest Raccoon Dies', *The Spokesman-review* (13 May 2004), www.spokesman.com.

12 Larry Woody, 'Whatever Happened to Rebekah the Raccoon?', *HartsvilleVidette.com* (1 August 2018), www.hartsvillevidette.com.

13 CNNWire, 'Two Michigan Children Attacked by Neighbor's Pet Raccoon' (11 May 2019), https://fox8.com.

14 Bill Wasik and Monica Murphy, *Rabid: A Cultural History of the World's Most Diabolical Virus* (New York, 2013), pp. 226–7.

15 Fernanda Santos, 'After Bedbugs, Here Come the Raccoons', *New York Times* online (30 August 2010), https://cityroom.blogs.nytimes.com.

16 Ernest Thompson Seton, *Wild Animal Ways* (Garden City, NY, 1922), p. 118.

17 Tohru Ikeda, Makoto Asano, Yohei Matoba and Go Abe, 'Present Status of Invasive Alien Raccoon and Its Impact in Japan', *Global Environmental Research*, VIII/2 (2004), p. 126.

18 Takaaki Suzuki and Tohru Ikeda, 'Challenges in Managing Invasive Raccoons in Japan', *Wildlife Research* (2019), CSIRO, p. A.

19 Ibid., p. 125.

20 Ibid., pp. A–B.

21 Ibid., p. 127.

22 'Raccoons Gone Wild: Background Reading', PBS LearningMedia, WNET (Boston, MA, 2013).

23 Suzuki and Ikeda, 'Challenges in Managing Invasive Raccoons in Japan', p. F; Harumi Akiba, Craig A. Miller and Hiroyuki Matsuda, 'Factor Influencing Public Preference for Raccoon Eradication Plan in Kanagawa, Japan', *Human Dimensions of Wildlife*, XVII/3 (2012), p. 208.

24 Matthias Schulz, 'Raccoon Invasion – Germany Overrun by Hordes of Masked Omnivores', *Spiegel Online International* (3 August 2012), www.spiegel.de.

25 Clara Guibourg, 'Sweden Fears Swimming Danish Raccoon Invasion', *The Local* online (23 August 2011), www.thelocal.se.

26 Stephen Burgen, 'Madrid Declares War on Plague of Raccoon and Parrot Invaders', *The Guardian* online (22 July 2013), www.theguardian.com.

27 Meghan Bartels, 'Germany Is Overrun with Raccoons – and the Rest of the Continent Is Worried They'll Be Next', *Business Insider* online (7 June 2016), www.businessinsider.com.

28 Vera Illugadóttir, 'Raccoons in Iceland: A Sad History', *Reykjavík Grapevine* (11 July 2014), www.grapevine.is.

29 Jesús T. García et al., 'Recent Invasion and Status of the Raccoon (*Procyon lotor*) in Spain', *Biological Invasions*, XIV (2012), pp. 1306, 1309.

30 Farman Fatullaevich Alieve and Glen C. Sanderson, 'Distribution and Status of the Raccoon in the Soviet Union', *Journal of Wildlife Management*, XXX/3 (July 1996), p. 500.

31 Azita Farashi, Mohammad Kaboli and Mahmoud Karami, 'Predicting Range Expansion of Invasive Raccoons in Northern Iran using ENFA Model at Two Different Scales', *Ecological Informatics*, XV (2013), p. 97.

32 Azita Farashi, Morteza Naderi and Sanaz Safavian, 'Predicting the Potential Invasive Range of Raccoons in the World', *Polish Journal of Ecology*, LXIV (2016), p. 596.

EPILOGUE: ARAKUN TRIUMPHANT?

1 Polly Redford, 'Our Most American Animal', *Harper's Magazine* (1 October 1963), pp. 47–8.
2 Steven R. Boyett, *The Architect of Dreams* (New York, 1986), p. 20.
3 Ibid., p. 42.
4 Amanda Phuong, 'Hilarious Nike Campaign Tackles Toronto's Raccoon Problem' (13 May 2015), www.styledemocracy.com.
5 Jim Rankin, *Raccoons: Everything You Always Wanted to Know about Them but Were Too Busy Cleaning Up Their Mess to Ask* (Toronto, 2013), p. 17.
6 Leyland Cecco, 'Raccoons vs. Toronto: How "Trash Pandas" Conquered the City', *The Guardian* (5 October 2018), www.theguardian.com.
7 Albrecht I. Schulte-Hostedde et al., 'Enhanced Access to Anthropogenic Food Waste Is Related to Hyperglycemia in Raccoons (*Procyon lotor*)', *Conservation Physiology*, VI/1 (2018), accessed 30 August 2019.
8 Amy Lavender Harris, 'Raccoon City', *The Puritan* (Summer 2014), www.puritan-magazine.com.

Select Bibliography

Arsznov, Bradley M., and Sharleen T. Sakai, 'The Procyonid Social Club:
  Comparison of Brain Volumes in the Coatimundi (*Nasua nasua,
  N. narica*), Kinkajou (*Potos flavus*), and Raccoon (*Procyon lotor*)',
  Brain, Behavior and Evolution, LXXXII/2 (October 2013), pp. 129–45
Audubon, John James, and John Bachman, *The Viviparous Quadrupeds
  of North America*, vol. II (New York, 1845)
Bateman, P. W., and P. A. Fleming, 'Big City Life: Carnivores in Urban
  Environments', *Journal of Zoology*, CCLXXXVII (2012), pp. 1–23
Beahrs, Andrew, *Twain's Feast: Searching for America's Lost Foods in the
  Footsteps of Samuel Clemens* (New York, 2010)
Eastman, Charles Alexander, 'Wechah the Provider', *Red Hunters and
  the Animal People* (New York, 2004), pp. 66–88
Farashi, Azita, Morteza Naderi and Sanaz Safavian, 'Predicting the
  Potential Invasive Range of Raccoons in the World', *Polish Journal
  of Ecology*, LXIV (2016)
Fischman, Lisa Anne, 'Coonskin Fever: Frontier Adventures in Postwar
  American Culture', unpublished PhD thesis, University
  of Minnesota, 1996
Gehrt, Stanley D., 'Raccoon', in *Wild Mammals of North America*
  (Baltimore, MD, 2003), pp. 611–34
Guardians of the Galaxy, written and directed by James Gunn, Marvel
  Studios (2014)
Harris, Amy Lavender, 'Raccoon City', *The Puritan* (Summer 2014),
  www.puritan-magazine.com
Holmgren, Virginia C., *Raccoons: In History, Folklore and Today's
  Backyards* (Santa Barbara, CA, 1990)

Hunter, Luke, *Carnivores of the World* (Princeton, NJ, 2011)

Ikeda, Tohru, Makoto Asano, Yohei Matoba and Go Abe, 'Present Status of Invasive Alien Raccoon and Its Impact in Japan', *Global Environmental Research*, VIII/2 (2004), pp. 125–31

Koepfli, Klaus-Peter, et al., 'Phylogeny of the Procyonidae (Mammalia: Carnivora): Molecules, Morphology and the Great American Interchange', *Molecular Phylogenetics and Evolution*, XLIII (2007), pp. 1076–95

Le Zotte, Jennifer, *From Goodwill to Grunge: A History of Secondhand Styles and Alternative Economies* (Chapel Hill, NC, 2017)

Lewis, Barbara, 'Daddy Blue: The Evolution of the Dark Dandy', in *Inside the Minstrel Mask: Readings in Nineteenth Century Black Minstrelsy*, ed. Annemarie Bean, James Hatch and Brooks McNamara (Hanover, NH, 1996)

McClearn, Deedra, 'Locomotion, Posture, and Feeding Behaviour of Kinkajous, Coatis, and Raccoons', *Journal of Mammalogy*, LXXIII/2 (May 1992), pp. 245–61

MacClintock, Dorcas, *A Natural History of Raccoons* (Caldwell, NJ, 2002)

Mantlo, Bill, and Mike Mignola, *Rocket Raccoon: Guardian of the Keystone Quadrant* (Kent, 2014)

Packer, Sharon, 'Halfworld's Loonies in *Rocket Raccoon* Comics – Serious or Satire?', in *Mental Illness in Popular Culture*, ed. Sharon Packer (Santa Barbara, CA, 2017)

Pettit, Michael, 'The Problem of Raccoon Intelligence in Behaviourist America', *British Journal for the History of Science*, XLIII/3 (September 2010), pp. 391–421

Proctor, Nicholas W., *Bathed in Blood: Hunting and Mastery in the Old South* (Charlottesville, VA, 2002)

Raccoon Nation, dir. Susan K. Fleming, written by Siobhan Flanagan, Rubin Tarrant Productions (2012)

Rawls, Wilson, *Where the Red Fern Grows* [1961] (New York, 2016)

Redford, Polly, 'Our Most American Animal', *Harper's Magazine* (1 October 1963), pp. 47–50

Schaefer, Jack, *An American Bestiary: Notes of an Amateur Naturalist* (Boston, MA, 1975)

Schroeder, Patricia, 'Passing for Black: Coon Songs and the Performance of Race', *Journal of American Culture*, XXXIII/2 (June 2010), pp. 139–53

Seton, Ernest Thompson, *Life-histories of Northern Animals* (New York, 1909)

—, *Wild Animal Ways* (Garden City, NY, 1922)

Suzuki, Takaaki, and Tohru Ikeda, 'Challenges in Managing Invasive Raccoons in Japan', *Wildlife Research* (2019), CSIRO

Tuan, Yi-Fu, *Dominance and Affection: The Making of Pets* (New Haven, CT, 1984)

Wasik, Bill, and Monica Murphy, *Rabid: A Cultural History of the World's Most Diabolical Virus* (New York, 2013)

Williams, Roland Leander Jr, *Black Male Frames: African Americans in a Century of Hollywood Cinema, 1903–2003* (Syracuse, NY, 2014)

Zeveloff, Samuel I., *Raccoons: A Natural History* (Washington, DC, 2002)

Websites and Organizations

ANIMAL DIVERSITY WEB
https://animaldiversity.org

CANADIAN WILDLIFE FEDERATION
http://cwf-fcf.org

THE GABLE'S RACCOON WORLD
www.raccoonworld.com

NATIONAL WILDLIFE FEDERATION (U.S.)
www.nwf.org

PBS NATURE: RACCOON NATION
www.pbs.org

RACCOON TRACKS
https://fohn.net

UNIVERSITY OF WYOMING RACCOON PROJECT
http://animalcognitionlab.org/raccoon

Acknowledgements

This book was envisioned, researched and written on the lands of the Musqueam and shíshálh peoples. I have benefited deeply from their hospitality, their teachings and their ongoing guardianship of these lands and waters I now call home. Galiheliga – I am grateful.

I want to thank all the co-organizers and participants in AnimalFest 2015, without whom this book would not exist: Rachel Poliquin (co-organizer and author of *Beaver*), Jonathan Burt (series editor and author of *Rat*), Graham Barwell (*Albatross*), Victoria de Rijke (*Duck*), Deirdre Jackson (*Lion*), Brent Mizelle (*Pig*), Martin Wallen (*Fox*), Victoria Dickenson (*Rabbit*), Annie Potts (*Chicken*), Alan Rauch (*Dolphin*), Philip Armstrong (*Sheep*), Robert Bieder (*Bear*), Susan McHugh (*Dog*), John Simons (*Kangaroo*) and John Sorenson (*Ape*), along with the following: Vin Nardizzi, Tiffany Werth, Tina Loo, Julie Andreyev, Daniel Hiebert, June Scudeler and Margery Fee (later author of *Polar Bear*); the UBC Oecologies Research Cluster; and my staff, faculty and student colleagues in the departments of English and history, First Nations and Indigenous Studies, the Social Justice Institute and the Critical Studies in Sexuality Program, the Science and Technology Studies Graduate Program, the UBC Beaty Biodiversity Museum and its staff (especially Ildiko Szabo, author of *Kingfisher*), Green College, the Vancouver Public Library and Heirloom Restaurant.

I am deeply indebted to the wonderfully skilled and encouraging team at Reaktion Books for their support, guidance, and professionalism at all points of the process. Particular appreciation goes to Jonathan Burt (again!), Michael Leaman, Phoebe Colley, Susannah Jayes, Maria Kilcoyne, Fran Roberts, Alex Ciobanu and Simon McFadden. Wado – thank you.

So many people have contributed to this book in ways small and large, including star indexer Emily LeGrand, my research assistants Ya'el Frankel, Lauren McClanaghan and Dylan Bateman, Irene Davy at the Gibsons Wildlife Rehabilitation Centre (who let me feed the irrepressible Blondie), Deanna Kreisel and Scott MacKenzie (for directing me to Rackety Coon Chile), Jenna Hunnef (for making me think so much about outlaws), Darlene Johnston (for the *Codex Canadiensis* materials), Jane Bowers (for knowledge and shared love of wildlife), Jill Campbell of the Musqeam Indian Band Language and Culture Department and the UBC Musqueam Language Program (for permission to use the Musqueam name for raccoon – *məlləs* – in the book), and Patrick Del Percio (for invaluable Cherokee language translation). My apologies for anyone I have missed in this list, but please know how much you are appreciated.

Very special thanks go to T. J. Tallie, Ayesha Chaudry, Rumee Ahmed, So Mayer, Kerry Goring and Patty Crawec for their review of Chapter Three in its various iterations, for their detailed critical feedback and for their encouragement. Suzanne MacDonald and Andrea Routley read the whole manuscript and offered important revision suggestions that made the book immeasurably better. Any errors, omissions or misrepresentations in the text are entirely my own responsibility. Gajiyali'elicheha digwali'i.

My mother, Kathy Justice, is my constant cheerleader and my best editor. She always knows just what I need along the way on any project. For *Raccoon* she supplied me with a surprise set of raccoon accessories to inspire me on the last big push with the book. Jiyali'elicheha eji.

My husband, Kent Dunn, is an endless source of enthusiasm, support, patience and editorial wisdom. Without him and his love none of this work would be possible. And in spite of my frequent distraction by endless bits of raccoonish minutiae, he always encouraged me and believed it was a worthy project. Jiyali'elicheha osdineli.

I lost a few close relatives in the last year of writing this book, but the deepest loss was my father, Jimmie J Justice, from whom I learned so much about what it is to care about this world and its other-than-human inhabitants. Thanks for those lessons, Dad, and for the love. I miss you every day. Jiyali'elicheha edoda jigesv'i.

Photo Acknowledgements

The author and publishers wish to express their thanks to the below sources of illustrative material and/or permission to reproduce it.

Alamy: pp. 50 (Carver Mostardi), 64 (SuperStock), 95 (Nature Picture Library); Art Resource, NY: pp. 63 (Erich Lessing), 107 (Metropolitan Museum of Art, NY), 118 (Andrew Wyeth, *Faraway*, 1952 © Estate of Andrew Wyeth/Socan, 2020); © *Boys' Life Magazine*/Boy Scouts of America: p. 71; CALVIN AND HOBBES © 2017 Watterson. Reprinted with permission of ANDREWS MCMEEL SYNDICATION. All rights reserved: p. 114; College of Arms UK: p. 156. Reproduced by permission of the Kings, Heralds and Pursuivants of Arms. College of Arms MS Grants [refs. nos. as listed]: D. C. Holmes (Grants 142, p 281), C. E. Edgar (Grants 147, p 169), C.W.G. Portal-Foster (Grants 148, p 348), J.W.H. Silvester (Grants 129, p 54); Rob Collinet: p. 183; Cornell University Library: p. 88 (Susan H. Douglas Collection of Political Americana); Photo by Brittany Crossman, http://www.brittanycrossman.com: p. 6; Used with permission of *Field & Stream* Copyright © 2020. All rights reserved: p. 158; Flickr Creative Commons (All images CC BY 2.0): pp. 18 Cathy Taylor (MissChatter), 28 David Slater (davrozs), 32 Rusty Clark (rusty_clark), 36 Fil.Al (fbohac), 169 Sarah Sapp (sghsapp), 170 Paulo O (brownpau), 175 Woody Hibbard (pamwood707), 177 Sam May, 182 Kitty Terwolbeck (kittysfotos); Sacha Ye Gauthier, www.windhoverphotography.com: p. 189; Getty Images: pp. 123 (Fred W. McDarrah), 128 (Kansas City Star), 142 (Silver Screen Collection), 148 (Carl Court/Stringer), 164 (Wisconsin Historical Society), 184 (Cole Burston); Gilcrease Museum: p. 31; Courtesy of The Linda Hall Library of Science, Engineering, and Technology/Jon

Rollins, Digital Initiatives Graphic Design Technician: pp. 21, 22; Photo by Matt Hansen, www.matthansenphotography.com: p. 48; John Hay Library, Brown University: p. 98; Images courtesy of Hennepin County Library: pp. 116, 117; iStockphoto: p. 3 (GlobalP); Kenan Research Center at the Atlanta History Center: p. 115; Library of Congress, Prints & Photographs Division: pp. 91 (LC-USZ62-30524), 100 (LC-USZ62-91410), 103, 120 (LC-USZ62-29198), 162 (Harris & Ewing Collection), 165, 168; Mary Evans Picture Library: p. 186 (© The Pictures Now Image Collection); Mathers Museum of World Cultures, Indiana University: p. 57; State Historical Society of Missouri Digital Collections: p. 13; Kent Monkman: p. 124; Monroe Historical Society, Monroe, Ohio: p. 133 (Marion G Warner Glass Plate Negative Collection); National Museum of American History, Smithsonian Institution: p. 86; National Wildlife Federation: p. 154 (images are published with the permission of the copyright owner, the National Wildlife Federation®); New York State Archives: pp. 153, 171; James Ng, JamesNgArt.com: p. 187; Barbara Norfleet: p. 181 (Chrysler Museum of Art, Norfolk, VA; gift of Joyce F. and Robert B. Menschel); Courtesy of the Ohio History Connection: pp. 54, 89; Copyright © Okefenokee Glee & Perloo, Inc. Used by permission: p. 150; Pennsylvania Game Commission: p. 155; Historical Society of Pennsylvania (Cartoons and Caricatures Collection): p. 92; Philadelphia Museum of Art: p. 113 (Gift of the McNeil Americana Collection, 2006, 2006-3-161); Pixabay: pp. 8 louisasimsrealtor, 34 Mona El Falaky (Cairomoon), 45 StockSnap, 46 Herbert Aust (herbert2512); Vadim Poleshchuk: p. 178; Jereldine Redcorn: p. 52 (Jereldine Redcorn, artist; courtesy of Smithsonian Institution, National Museum of Natural History, Department of Anthropology; catalogue number E432917; photo by James Di Loreto); Sandra and Woo (www.sandraandwoo.com), © Powree and Oliver Knörzer. Used by permission: p. 151; Shutterstock: p. 143 (Moviestore); Photograph © 2020 courtesy of The David and Alfred Smart Museum of Art, The University of Chicago: p. 62; Diagram by Derek Tan, Beatty Biodiversity Museum, UBC: p. 20 (Kinkajou: Ichtusvet on Wikimedia Commons, CC BY-SA 4.0; Raccoon: Jennifer C on Flickr, CC BY 2.0; Ringtail: Robert Body on Wikimedia Commons, CC BY-SA 3.0; Olingo: Jeremy Gatten on Flickr, CC BY-SA 2.0; Coati: Neil McIntosh on Flickr, CC BY 2.0);

Index

Page numbers in *italics* indicate illustrations